Plants

Christine Shaw

First published in 2005 by Collins
an imprint of HarperCollins*Publishers*
77–85 Fulham Palace Road, London W6 8JB

everything clicks at:
www.collins.co.uk

Text by Christine Shaw, © HarperCollins*Publishers*
Photography, artworks and design © HarperCollins*Publishers*

Photography by Christine Shaw and Tim Sandall

Based on material from the *Collins Practical Gardener* series

Project Editor: Claire Musters
Designer: Helen Taylor
Indexer: Katie Hardwicke

For HarperCollins:

Senior Managing Editor: Angela Newton
Editor: Alastair Laing
Art Direction: Luke Griffin

Collins Gem® is a registered trademark of
HarperCollinsPublishers

A CIP catalogue record for this book is available from the
British Library

ISBN 0 00 720124 9

Colour reproduction by Digital Imaging

Printed and bound by Amadeus S.r.l., Italy

CONTENTS

Phyllostachys nigra

INTRODUCTION

For a plant to be architectural, it has to have either a very strong shape or a very strong presence in the garden. There are obvious examples, such as palms, while others are much more understated – providing perhaps a shapely outline when mature. There are also bold, brash plants that demand attention. These can all be combined to create many different looks, from a wild jungle to a Japanese garden.

Architectural plants are hugely popular today as many people want to grow something exotic in their gardens. This book offers you all the information you need on a large selection of the top architectural specimens.

Beschorneria yuccoides

HOW TO USE THIS BOOK

This book is divided into two parts. The first chapter guides you through the basic care of architectural plants. The majority of the book is given over to the directory, which provides individual entries on the best architectural plants to grow, listed alphabetically by Latin name. The example entry below is annotated to show you what information each section provides.

The Latin name of the plant, followed by its common name where relevant

KEY FACTS give basic information on the type of site and climate the plant needs, covering:

Min temp: the lowest temperature the plant can tolerate
Soil: the best soil for growing in terms of nutrients, drainage and chemical content
Site: whether to plant in a sunny, shady or part-shaded position, and the degree of shelter required
Vigour: indicates how fast the plant grows and, where relevant, gives the maximum height and spread

CARE The care box gives specific information on feeding, watering and pruning requirements as well as indicating what pests and diseases the plant is prone to

ARCHITECTURAL PLANT CARE

As with all plants, architectural specimens need to be looked after. This chapter gives you all the information you need to plan and care for your architectural garden.

CHOOSING PLANTS

Knowing what type of garden you have in terms of shade, sun, available moisture, soil pH and fertility will help you to choose the right plants. However, there are a few other things you should consider too.

Impact

If you like to watch plants grow then you will be able to save money by choosing tiny seedlings, and gain satisfaction from nurturing them through to maturity. However, you will have to wait several years for your garden to take shape. On the other hand, if you want to create an instant display you will need to buy maturer specimens, which will be more expensive.

Dicksonia antarctica
makes a bold statement.

Maintenance

The kind of life you lead should have a direct bearing on the type of garden to aim for. If you have plenty of free time, you can grow plants that demand regular attention. If, however, you lead a busy life, choose low maintenance plants. This

Agaves are generally low maintenance.

doesn't mean your garden has to be dull – there are many lovely yet virtually maintenance-free plants.

Cost

Getting to know how quickly plants reach maturity will help you plan what to buy. If you want a eucalyptus, for example, it is so fast-growing that to spend money on a large plant is pointless. On the other hand, palms are so slow-growing that buying a small plant could be frustrating.

Another consideration is the size of a plant in relation to its hardiness. For example, desert-type plants such as agaves can better cope with cold, wet winters if they are at least 60cm (2ft) tall. It is worth spending a little extra on a more mature plant, if a younger plant is less likely to withstand the conditions in your garden.

Plants in containers

Growing plants in containers is a good option if you have a small garden area that is paved or on a balcony or roof. Containers are also useful for filling bare patches in the garden. A plant in a container will stand out more too.

Containers add variety to a garden.

THE RIGHT SHAPE
The traditional flowerpot has a carefully chosen shape. It is wide at the top, narrow at the bottom and has smooth, straight sides, which means that however potbound a plant becomes, it can be pulled out.

SUITABLE PLANTS FOR POTS
There are two categories of architectural plants that grow well in containers. The first is slow-growing plants such as *Chamaerops humilis*. The other is desert plants, which can cope with periods of drought, hot sun during the day and freezing temperatures at night.

TIP: Always ensure there is good drainage in a container – such as broken ceramics in the bottom and a large drainage hole. Also remember to water container plants regularly.

GROWING CONDITIONS

Before you buy any plants, you should assess your garden. The information given on the plants in the directory includes the best place to grow them so you need to know what conditions your garden provides.

Assessing your garden

Walk around your garden at different points in the day, noting areas of sun or shade. After heavy rain, find out which areas retain water and which dry out fast, and whether or not there is good drainage overall.

SOIL

You need to know whether the soil is acid or alkaline and what level of fertility it offers. Alkaline soil has a high lime content and some plants do not perform well in it. Kits are available from garden centres to test for alkalinity. Fortunately, soil fertility can be altered as some plants are greedy and need feeding with a fertiliser.

EXPOSURE
Take note of how much your garden is exposed to the wind. A sheltered garden will allow you to grow almost any plant.

Check for alkaline soil using a pH test kit.

What to grow where

Each garden is different, with its own specific, prevailing conditions to take into account. However there are a number of elements that usually feature in most gardens, and you will almost certainly need to take the same factors into account when assessing the suitability of your garden for the cultivation of your favourite architectural plants. Here is a quick guide to what plants grow best, and also what to avoid planting, in various conditions.

A gradient Avoid planting delicate plants on a gradient.

Damp, low corner This is an ideal spot for bamboos, gunnera and moisture-loving plants.

Higher, free-draining ground Particularly good for sun-loving desert plants.

Permanently shady area beneath a tree A good spot for shade-loving plants.

Sheltered, shady area, out of the sun all day Ideal for ferns and fatsias.

Sheltered, sunny border Ideal for sun-loving plants.

Windy corner Avoid planting large-leafed specimens here.

PLANTING COMBINATIONS

There are many different planting combinations you may like to consider, depending of course on the conditions in your garden.

Jungle combinations

For damp, slightly shady gardens with rich, fertile soil, creating a jungle look is easy.

Example plants: *Acanthus mollis, Arundinaria anceps, Bilbergia nutans, Canna indica, Canna iridiflora, Chamaerops humilis, Dicksonia antarctica, Eryngium agavifolium, Fatshedera lizei, Fatsia japonica, Gunnera manicata, Kniphofia northiae, Musa basjoo, Phormium tenax, Sasa palmata nebulosa, Zantedeschia aethiopica* 'Crowborough'.

Desert combinations

For sun-baked gardens with free-draining soil, desert-type plants are ideal.

Example plants: *Agave americana, Agave salmiana* var. 'Ferox', *Beschorneria yuccoides, Brahea armata, Butia capitata, Colletia cruciata, Dasylirion acrotrichum, Echeveria glauca, Euphorbia myrsinites, Kniphofia caulescens, Puya chilensis, Sempervivum* spp., *Yucca aloifolia, Yucca glauca*.

Mediterranean-style combinations

A typical Mediterranean garden is sunny and well-drained, provides some form of shelter in the summer and has scented plants and vibrant flowers.

Example plants: *Albizia julibrissin, Cynara cardunculus, Eucalyptus niphophila* 'Debeuzevillei', *Ficus carica, Iris confusa, Ligustrum lucidum, Pinus pinea, Rosmarinus repens.*

Seaside combinations

Gardening on the coast is extremely challenging. Use plants with dense foliage, under-planted with salt-resistant ground cover.

Example plants: *Aloe striatula, Cordyline australis, Eucalyptus aggregata, Euphorbia wulfenii, Ophiopogon planiscapus* 'Nigrescens', *Phormium cookianum, Yucca gloriosa.*

Japanese combinations

Quiet and calm, Japanese gardens often have water with just a few carefully chosen specimens.

Example plants: *Aralia elata, Clematis armandii, Phyllostachys nigra, Pittosporum tobira, Podocarpus salignus.*

PLANTING

While it is straightforward to plant specimens, there is a certain amount of preparation needed.

Preparing the soil

First, check that the soil is fertile enough to support what you intend growing. If plants need rich soil and yours is lacking, dig in well-rotted manure or blood, fish and bone. Also check the soil has the correct moisture content. If it is too dry, consider installing automatic irrigation. If the soil is too wet, dig over the site to incorporate as much grit, hardcore or gravel as you can so that excess rain will drain away rather than collect.

Planting into the ground

It is important to plant trees, shrubs and herbaceous plants at the correct depth. The amount of root under the ground must be exactly the same as when the plant was in its pot. If placed too low, water can get into the central growth point and create rotting. If placed too high, surface roots could be left exposed to the air – these will dry out quickly and die.

PLANTING A TREE

Gently remove the young tree from its container. Dig a hole slightly larger than the container, using it as a guide (1). Loosen the soil at the bottom of the hole and sprinkle in a handful of bonemeal. Place the tree into the hole so it is straight. Replace the soil into the hole and firm it down (2).

Take three 1.8m (6ft) stakes and tie kits, and hammer them 60cm (2ft) into the ground 120° apart around the tree (3). Using three stakes ensures nothing is hammered through the roots, whatever direction the wind is blowing the bark won't rub against the stakes and it will be hard to damage the tree.

1 Dig a hole, using the pot as a size guide.

2 Gently replace the soil into the hole.

3 Tie the tree to each of the stakes.

TIP: The technique for planting up all other plants is similar to that for trees, but there is usually no need for supporting stakes. If you are planting a desert plant that likes dry, free-draining soil, add a thin layer of grit to the bottom of the hole.

Planting containers

With the exception of tree ferns, the same soil mix can be used for all container plants – John Innes No. 3, plus up to 50% extra grit stirred in. John Innes composts are loam-based, providing balanced nutrients over a long period; No. 3 means it has the greatest amount of fertilisers. Adding grit makes it free-draining.

To replant a specimen into a pot, position the plant and add John Innes No. 3 with extra grit. Fill to just below the rim and then finish off with a layer of gravel on top of the compost to prevent drying out.

Position the plant in the pot then add the compost.

Put a layer of gravel on the top to prevent drying out.

FEEDING

Specific feeding requirements for each plant are given in the directory, but here are some general tips.

When to feed

Plants can only absorb food when they are growing. This is usually, but not always, during spring. If you are creating new areas in the garden, however, it makes sense to incorporate food while preparing them.

What to use

Knowing the main constituents, and understanding how each chemical benefits a particular area of the plant, will help determine your choice of fertiliser.

Nitrogen Leafy plants need this to stay lush and green.

Potash This helps plants to flower and fruit.

Phosphates This helps the root system to grow and is most beneficial to trees and shrubs.

> **TIP:** If feeding individual plants in the spring, use a concentrated organic fertiliser, such as a blood, fish and bone mixture. If any plant needs a top-up in the summer, add some liquid fertiliser to each can of water.

WATERING

There is no easy rule that says how much and how often to water. Several factors must be considered.

Growth While a plant is growing, it needs regular watering. When dormant, it doesn't need much water.

Weather Watering is obviously a necessity in hot weather. But even in winter, if it hasn't rained much newly planted trees and bamboos will need water.

Soil type The amount of water that can be held in soil depends on its structure. Soil with small particles, such as clay, can hold large amounts of moisture while larger particles such as chalk hold on to far less.

Pot plants Plants grown in containers require far more watering than those planted in the ground.

Drought-resistant plants With such plants, this quality only applies after they are established, so they will still need watering in dry weather when young.

TIP: Apart from not watering, the next worst thing you can do is to water often using very small quantities as most of the water evaporates off rather than reaching the roots.

SUPPORT

We have already seen that young trees need supporting with a stake (*see* p. 14). Many climbers also need support. There are two main types of climbing architectural plants: self-clinging and those that require trellis or wire support. Self-clinging climbers produce aerial roots that will hang onto rough surface so there is no need to tie them in. Other climbers wind around trellis or wires attached to a fence. These must be tied in. Their new shoots all grow upwards to the sun and will need to be tied in regularly.

Tie in new shoots as they appear.

WEEDING

A weed can be any plant growing where it isn't wanted. Here are some tips to help speed up your weeding:

- Mulching involves spreading gravel, bark or pebbles on top of soil. This helps prevent weed seeds growing.
- Weed regularly.
- Hoeing gets rid of annual weeds, but not perennials.
- Weeding by hand, with the help of a fork, is more efficient for getting rid of perennial weed roots.

PRUNING

This is done to keep a plant neat and tidy or to control its size (*see also* brown-bitting, pp 22–3). It can involve removing any dead wood or branches growing in the wrong direction, or thinning out a plant if too many branches have been produced. Here are a few basic points to remember when pruning:

Sharp secateurs help you make neat cuts.

- Deciduous plants (those that lose their leaves in the autumn) should be pruned when they are dormant.
- Evergreen plants need to be pruned according to when they flower. So summer-flowering plants should be tidied up in late spring before buds form. Early-flowering plants should be pruned as soon as they finish flowering in early spring.
- Plants grown for their foliage only can be pruned any time during the growing season.
- Herbaceous (non-woody) plants should be cut right back to the ground after the first frosts have scorched their leaves.
- Container plants should be clipped little and often throughout the growing season so they are kept in a controlled shape suitable for their containers.

WINTER PROTECTION

It is best to grow only plants appropriate for the local climate, but you may find a few vulnerable plants too irresistible. To ensure survival, wrap them up in winter.

When to wrap?

This all depends on the climate and the hardiness of the plant. Find out the minimum temperature for the area during winter and compare this with what the plant can cope with. Then listen to the weather forecast!

Wrapping a plant

The majority of plants that need protection can be covered using the method shown here. Scoop up the foliage and tie it with string to keep it together (1).

1 Tie the foliage with string.

2 Wrap the fleece around the plant.

3 Tie the fleece into place.

This ensures all the younger growth inside is fully protected. Wrap several layers of agricultural fleece around the plant (2). (This can be bought from most garden centres.) Secure it with string and cut off the fleece from the roll. Tie the fleece in several places to prevent winter gales from blowing it away (3).

Protecting tree ferns

Tree ferns need protection during the winter months and cannot simply be covered in fleece. Those grown in pots can be moved somewhere frost-free for the winter, such as a greenhouse. For those in the ground, there are two possible methods of protection:

- Wait until the fronds have frosted and gone brown, then cut them off close to the trunk. The most vulnerable part of the plant is then at the tip of the trunk. To keep this area frost-free, gently push straw or hessian into it, and fasten with string (*see* picture).
- Get hold of a decent number of straw bales. Pull up the fronds vertically and secure them with string. Then stack the bales as tightly as possible around the trunk, gradually building them up to conceal both trunk and fronds.

Push straw into the tip of the trunk to protect it.

BROWN-BITTING

Brown-bitting involves manicuring foliage by literally removing all the brown bits. This makes such a difference to the appearance of architectural plants that it should be regarded as an integral part of their general care. The best time of year to do it is late spring/early summer, when plants are growing.

Basic technique

Starting with the older lower leaves, take a sharp knife or pair of secateurs, pull the leaf taut and cut as near to the stem as possible (1). Gradually work your way up the trunk (2). When every brown leaf has been trimmed off (3), remove any old flower stems.

1 Cut as close to the stem as you can.

2 Gradually work your way up the trunk.

3 Continue until every brown leaf has gone.

TIP: Always use secateurs or scissors that have been fully sharpened. Never pull leaves off, as doing this can rip into the delicate layer of the stem and do a great deal of harm (it's like cutting finger nails too far down into the cuticle).

Trimming palm leaves

Palms can have their old, dangling, yellow and brown foliage cut right back using the same basic technique. However, each individual leaf can also be manicured, which sounds an incredibly time-consuming project, but is definitely worthwhile.

Fan palms often have brown tips that form at the ends of leaves. Lightly trimming the ends can extend the smart appearance of a palm fan by several months. Try to cut as straight as you can. If you trim the fans of your palm regularly, leaves may start to look too small after two or three trimmings. At this stage the entire fan should be chopped off, right back to the base of the leaf stalk. Be ruthless as you are not harming the plant. Removing the brown parts of a leaf will in fact encourage your palm to become an even healthier and stronger plant.

PESTS AND DISEASES

This section details some of the most common pests, diseases and cultivation problems and provides information on how to combat them.

Aphids These feed on the young growth of a plant, spreading viruses and depositing a sticky substance that can cause black, sooty mould. Apply organic insecticide regularly in the growing season. Ladybird beetles and larvae feed on pests such as aphids.

Green capsid The toxic saliva of this bug kills plant tissues, causing the leaves to eventually tear. Damage is not usually apparent until the insects have long gone. Apply organic insecticide regularly on plants likely to be attacked.

Growth problems If a plant is not flowering as it should, increase its dose of potash in the spring. Pale, undersized leaves are probably due to a nitrogen deficiency so feed the plant with a high-nitrogen feed. The plant may also be in a restricted surrounding, such as a container that is too small for the plant.

Leaf spot This fungal disease can spread through entire plants. Remove affected leaves immediately and burn them. Routinely drench any plants likely to suffer with a systemic fungicide containing copper, and improve drainage.

Mealy bugs White, furry masses of insects that cling to a plant and feed off the sap. Remove small numbers with a cotton wool bud dipped in methylated spirits. Ladybird beetles love this pest during warmer months. However, large colonies need a strong systemic insecticidal chemical.

Red spider mite Can affect most plants but rarely found on those grown outside. Main symptom is yellow mottling on leaves; in severe cases webs appear between top leaves. Treat with a chemical spray or introduce natural insect predators – the best is *Phytoseilus persimilis*. Prevention is the best remedy. Mites flourish in a hot, dry environment so increase humidity and improve ventilation.

Rotting Remove affected leaves before the rot spreads through the plant. In autumn, drench susceptible plants with a copper-based fungicide to try to prevent this occurring throughout the winter months. Ensure there is sufficient drainage.

Slugs and snails These enjoy eating most plants. As frogs and hedgehogs feed on these pests, do not poison them. Try to avoid using organic mulches, which encourage slugs and snails. Either collect them at night or use pellets that contain a slug repellent rather than killer.

Yellowing/brown leaves Caused by numerous things. Some plants do this naturally in autumn. However, plants that have been newly transplanted can suffer sudden, but short-lived, leaf drop. Otherwise a plant may be suffering from underwatering, lack of nutrients, the soil could be too alkaline or it could be waterlogged.

A–Z DIRECTORY OF PLANTS

This plant directory showcases the most commonly available architectural plants. Listed alphabetically by Latin name these include bamboos, grasses, ferns, palms, climbers, trees, spiky and succulent plants and other leafy exotics. From spectacular choices for tropical-looking gardens through to more delicate specimens with delightful scents, these pages will inspire you as you create your own garden – and give you the practical know-how to look after each plant.

ACACIA DEALBATA *Mimosa*

This evergreen tree is suitable for small gardens. Although the ferny foliage looks delicate, it thrives in coastal areas but some shelter is required from exposed sites. *A. dealbata* loves as much sun as it can get, so plant it against a sunny wall.

This tree is a popular choice for conservatories, as the scent from the flowers can fill the whole room. However, its speedy growth really makes it unsuitable for growing in a pot.

KEY FACTS

Min Temp -4°C (24°F)

Soil Poor, very well-drained and slightly acid. Chalky soil should be avoided

Site Full sun

Vigour Fast-growing, but with a maximum height of 8m (25ft)

CARE: Once established in the ground, this tree becomes extremely drought resistant. No feeding is required and pruning is only necessary if the tree becomes too large for its site. Outdoors it is usually trouble-free, but scale insects can be a problem under glass.

ACANTHUS MOLLIS

Bear's breeches or big spinach

The word 'mollis' is a lovely choice for this plant – it means soft or velvety in Latin, describing the leaves perfectly. Flower spikes are very stately, towering above the foliage in large numbers during midsummer. They are made up of flowers and bracts that are long-lasting and make good cut flowers for indoors – they are also suitable candidates for drying.

In an average climate, *Acanthus mollis* remains beautifully green all year round, making it an extremely architectural addition to any planting scheme. However, consider its position carefully. It detests root disturbance and will not usually survive being dug up and moved elsewhere.

KEY FACTS

Min Temp -20°C (-4°F)

Soil Although this plant can grow in any soil, rich loam is preferred

Site Sun or light shade. Keep sheltered from wind as this tears the large leaves easily

Vigour Has huge, soft leaves 60cm (2ft) long and 30cm (1ft) across with flowers up to 1.5m (5ft) in height above them

CARE: For best results, keep the soil moist, particularly during the growing season. Annual feeding each spring is also important. Remove any older yellow leaves, cutting right back to the base. They will quickly re-shoot and provide masses of fresh new growth. Watch out for slugs – *Acanthus mollis* is a haven for them.

AGAPANTHUS AFRICANUS   *African lily*

Although the large clumps of leathery strap-like leaves are attractive in their own right, it is for the enormous flower spikes that this plant is usually grown. Each stunning flower head is comprised of dozens of individual blossoms in either pure white or bright blue.

This plant is an unusual example of one that does better in a pot than it would if planted in the ground. The reason for this is that when it is grown within a container, it is easy to move under cover if the weather becomes too wet and cold.

KEY FACTS

Min Temp -4°C (24°F)

Soil Prefers rich, well-drained soil. Use John Innes No. 3 with extra grit if planting it in a container

Site This plant appreciates full sun or light shade out of strong winds

Vigour Has huge flower spikes, towering up to 1.5m (5ft) above the foliage and opening up into large balls that can reach 30cm (1ft) across

CARE: Water regularly during the growing season. Allow to dry out during the winter. Feed from spring onwards with regular doses of tomato food. After flowering, cut back the stems as low as you can. The plant does not generally suffer from many pests and diseases, apart from the occasional rogue slug.

AGAVE AMERICANA   *The Century plant*

A beautifully shaped plant that makes its presence loud and clear in the garden. Large, weighty leaves curve gently outwards forming an enormous tulip shape. They are blue-grey, have the appearance of being lightly dusted with white powder and are edged with painfully sharp spines. Each leaf ends in a long sharp needle. Flower spikes are extremely impressive but are unlikely to be seen on plants less than 25 years old. Some take as long as 40 years or more, but rarely as long as the 100 years that its common name suggests. The plant dies after flowering.

Agaves make excellent choices for growing in pots. Plants become much hardier once they reach 60cm (2ft) and will also cope with cold winters more successfully if kept dry. Good drainage is vital – planting on a sloping site helps with the drainage even more, as any rain can easily drain away instead of collecting in the central core of the plant.

KEY FACTS
Min Temp -4°C (24°F)
Soil Gritty and very sharply drained
Site Full sun – brilliant for exposed or sloping gardens
Vigour Growth is extremely slow. Over 30 years, *A. americana* could reach 1.5m x 1.5m (5ft x 5ft)

CARE: Water regularly from late spring to early autumn.
Keep fairly dry during the winter. Feed annually in spring
with a mix of blood, fish and bone. Do not get any on the
leaves, as they could become scorched. Watch out for slugs.
Roots and leaves will rot in wet conditions. Mealy bug can
be a problem on plants that are grown indoors.

AGAVE PARRYI

This plant has neatly arranged chunky foliage that forms a clump shaped like an artichoke. Leaves are blue-grey and tipped with sharp spines. It is the hardiest member of the whole *Agave* family. However, this hardiness depends on how dry the conditions are during the winter which, for many climates, is an unlikely occurrence. Cold and dry weather is fine but

cold and wet weather will quickly turn the plant into a soggy mess. For this reason, it is perhaps best to grow *A. parryi* in a large pot that can be brought under cover for the winter.

Although *Agave parryi* is rarely seen growing in groups in its native regions of Arizona and Mexico, specimens look most fetching and quite natural if planted this way in desert gardens.

KEY FACTS

Min Temp -10°C (14°F)

Soil Likes sharply drained soil with masses of added grit. Will grow in alkaline, neutral or acid soil

Site Full sun – best grown in a large pot unless the garden is very mild

Vigour Slow-growing – the whole plant rarely exceeds 45cm (1½ft) across and it can take 20 years to reach this size.

CARE: Water regularly during its growing season. Keep almost dry mid-autumn to early spring. Give the plant a light application of food, such as blood, fish and bone, annually in late spring. Watch out for slugs. Roots and leaves will rot in wet conditions. Mealy bug can be a problem on indoor plants.

AGAVE SALMIANA VAR. 'FEROX'

This vicious monster has large rigid leaves that are wide and flat, olive green in colour, edged with sharp hooks and ending with an astonishingly dangerous tip several inches long – truly the stuff of nightmares and absolutely one of the most fantastic plants in the whole world.

Although not very hardy, except in the mildest gardens, this plant is perfect for a windy coastal garden or roof terrace as it is virtually hurricane-proof. It is a good choice for growing in a large pot that can be moved under cover during the winter.

Away from its native country, Mexico, the plant is unlikely to flower. Offsets are occasionally produced – these should be removed and can be used for propagation or just thrown away.

CARE: Water regularly from late spring to early autumn. Allow to almost dry out mid-autumn until mid-spring. Feed annually in late spring with a mix of blood, fish and bone, taking care not to get any on the leaves. Mealy bug can be a problem. Roots and leaves can rot or suffer from fungal infections in cold, wet conditions.

KEY FACTS

Min Temp -4°C (24°F)

Soil Will grow in any soil that is exceptionally gritty and free-draining

Site Full sun, best on a slope or bank to aid drainage. Copes with exposed conditions well

Vigour Dimensions of a fully grown plant can reach 1.2m x 1.2m (4ft x 4ft)

ALBIZIA JULIBRISSIN   *Silk tree or pink siris*

This beautiful deciduous tree would be a stunning addition to any small garden. The large leaves look far too delicate for most climates but the plant has proved itself to be very tough indeed.

This tree comes into leaf rather late, usually around the end of spring, and it can start shedding its foliage as early as late summer. For this reason, it is best grown against a sunny wall where its season can be extended by several weeks. A sun-baked position produces copious amounts of pale pink powder-puff flowers in midsummer, which last for about six weeks. Long, green seedpods are occasionally produced after an especially hot summer.

Min Temp -20℃ (-4°F)
Soil Well-drained, poor soil that is neutral to slightly acid. Avoid planting *A. julibrissin* in chalky soil
Site Full sun, preferably against a warm wall to make full use of the sun
Vigour The plant's ultimate height could eventually reach a maximum of only 8m (25ft), which makes it suitable for even the smallest town garden

CARE: Once established, this tree becomes extremely drought resistant. It is virtually maintenance free – occasional light pruning can be done to keep the head a tidy, balanced shape. Coral spot can be a problem. Mature plants should be checked for this before buying.

ALOE ARISTATA

Hardy aloe

This clump-forming succulent has individual stemless rosettes of around 20cm (8in) across. The foliage is dark green and streaked with white dotted lines (known as tubercles) across each leaf. The fleshy foliage contains a lovely slimy gel that can be used to soothe burns, just like its more famous cousin, *Aloe vera*. Flower stems rise out of the centre of each rosette during the summer and last for many weeks. They are tall stems that open out into orange-red elongated bells.

A. aristata can be used in rockeries, gravel gardens, containers or planted out into any dry, sun-baked position. The plant looks especially attractive when it is planted into large, shallow, terracotta pots.

Aloe aristata is very easy to propagate from its offsets, which are produced by the plant in copious amounts.

KEY FACTS

Min Temp -10℃ (14°F)

Soil The plant thrives well in any soil that is gritty and sharply drained

Site Full sun is essential if it is to flower. Grows well in large, shallow pots

Vigour *A. aristata* is slow-growing and it can take eight years for a clump to spread 1m (3ft)

CARE: Provide a thorough monthly soaking from late spring to early autumn. Very little maintenance is necessary. A light feed once a year can be given if required. Pests and diseases are rarely a problem if grown outside. Under glass, however, mealy bug is an occasional visitor.

ALOE STRIATULA

This is an upright, branching succulent with long, pointed fleshy leaves that are full of thick, syrupy jelly. The flowers are stunning and usually produced in early summer. They are large, torch-shaped and bright yellow. These plants are hardy in most areas except really bad frost pockets. They perform particularly well in coastal gardens.

These plants need to be grown in the sunniest part of the garden and appreciate being against a warm wall, not only because this will make them flower more, but also because some support is needed to prop them up. They are so top heavy that, if planted in a pot or in the middle of a border, they will topple over with the weight of the foliage.

KEY FACTS

Min Temp -10°C (14°F)
Soil Any soil that is very well-drained. Extra grit could be added to the soil in order to provide even better drainage
Site Full sun in a sheltered spot, preferably against a wall for warmth and support
Vigour This plant can easily reach 1.2m (4ft) tall with a spread of 1m (3ft) after five years

CARE: New plants need watering but are drought resistant once established. Give an annual feed of blood, fish and bone, sprinkling it around the base in mid- or late spring. Remove older brown leaves. After flowering, cut off old flower spikes as low down as possible. Slugs adore these plants and can make unsightly scrapings along leaf surfaces.

ARALIA ELATA   *Japanese angelica tree*

This lovely Japanese tree has huge leaves that are over 1m (3ft) long, and beautifully crafted into delicate leaflets along the length of each stem. The plant is very hardy and, although deciduous, still makes a worthy contribution to any exotic garden. The slim, rarely straight trunk is covered with thorns even into maturity, making it rather an odd sight – especially in the winter after the leaves have dropped. Clusters of cream-coloured flowers appear in great profusion during late summer.

Although often seen as a multi-stemmed shrub, *Aralia elata* is far superior when it is grown as a single-stemmed tree. Suckers from the roots can be removed to keep the plant single-stemmed. These can be kept and used for propagation.

KEY FACTS
Min Temp -20°C (-4°F)
Soil Likes light, manure-enriched, free-draining soil
Site Woodland shade, preferably in a sheltered spot out of strong winds
Vigour A very slow-growing tree, with a maximum height of around 6m (20ft)

CARE: Keep soil moist for first few seasons. Fairly drought resistant when established. Feed annually in spring with a mix of blood, fish and bone. Prune back suckers to control spread. Capsid bugs can be very troublesome, so regular checks should be made for even the slightest damage.

ARAUCARIA ARAUCANA *Monkey puzzle tree*

This very peculiar-looking plant from Chile is totally unlike any other fully hardy tree. Its leaves are sharp blades that cover each branch as well as the full length of the trunk, while its branches are long and spidery. Cones are sometimes produced on older specimens and these contain edible seeds.

This evergreen conifer is excellent for planting on the coast in exposed positions as it is so wind resistant. Plant it so that it has plenty of space around it, in order for the beautiful shape to be appreciated. It is not a tree that can be moved easily if it is found to be growing in the wrong place. Plant one that is at least 60cm (2ft) tall, although this will be fairly expensive. This is a very variable plant – it is hard to find two examples that are exactly the same.

KEY FACTS

Min Temp -20°C (-4°F)

Soil Rich, moderately fertile, loamy soil, preferably moist but well-drained

Site Sunny – excellent in windy coastal gardens. Don't crowd it out with other plants

Vigour A very slow-growing tree, *Araucaria araucana* can eventually reach a height of 18m (60ft) over a period of about 100 years

CARE: Moist conditions are required, especially for the first few years after planting. Feed annually in mid-spring, with a mixture of blood, fish and bone sprinkled around the base. This plant is relatively trouble-free as pests and diseases do not usually cause any problems.

ARBUTUS x ANDRACHNOIDES

Red-barked strawberry tree

This evergreen tree has elegant, finely serrated leaves that mass together to form a dense head of foliage. It has amazing cinnamon-red wood, which peels from the branches and trunk in strips throughout the year, and large clusters of white, waxy bell-shaped flowers throughout most of the winter.

It is easy to grow this plant as it will tolerate most conditions. Staking for at least the first two years is vital (*see* p. 14). Also, buy a decent-sized tree with some visible red bark to ensure that the correct plant has been acquired – these trees are notorious for being wrongly labelled.

KEY FACTS

Min Temp -10°C (14°F)

Soil The plant will tolerate poor, even chalky, soil, as long as it is well-drained

Site Sunny position, preferably sheltered from very strong winds

Vigour Fast-growing when young, it is still a manageable tree for a small garden as it is unlikely to exceed 8m (25ft) even after several decades of growth

CARE: Give the plant plenty of water for the first couple of years until drought resistance develops. Feed annually in spring. Dropping of older leaves occurs in early spring. This should last for three to four weeks. Black fungal spots tend to develop on the foliage if the plant is waterlogged or confined to a pot for too long.

ARUNDINARIA ANCEPS *Himalayan bamboo*

Lovely cascades of soft, evergreen foliage make this bamboo very desirable. It can be grown either as a single specimen or massed together for screening. The leaves are so plentiful that it can even be trimmed to form a thick hedge. Flowering rarely occurs, which is a good thing as plants usually die afterwards.

Select a decently sized specimen for planting, as small seedlings are often extremely difficult to get going. Choose a sheltered site out of strong winds, as the more sheltered the planting position, the greener and healthier the foliage will look.

KEY FACTS

Min Temp -20°C (-4°F)
Soil Growing this plant in fertile, manure-enriched clay soil gives excellent results
Site Sun or light shade, and ideally in a sheltered position out of the wind
Vigour Fast-growing, this plant will fill a large space very quickly. Its maximum height is usually no more than 4–5m (13–16½ft)

CARE: It is crucial that this plant never dries out. Feeding is also important – every four weeks from mid-spring to early summer a few handfuls of a blood, fish and bone mix should be sprinkled around the base. If grown as a hedge, clip regularly throughout the growing season. Also check regularly throughout the same season for green aphids.

ASTELIA CHATHAMICA

Silver spear

This plant has the most remarkable colouring of silver on each leaf. Its sword-shaped leaves gently curve outwards and can reach a length of 1.5m (5ft). Flowers are disappointingly dull and therefore best removed as soon as they form.

The plant thrives on neglect and is quite happy in a pot that is infrequently watered. It is, however, best grown in the ground in a shady spot.

KEY FACTS
Min Temp -10°C (14°F)
Soil The plant will grow in virtually any soil, as long as it is very well-drained
Site It is happiest in light shade, but will tolerate most other conditions
Vigour Large, densely packed clumps can fill 1sq m (1sq ft) within five years

CARE: Watering and feeding are unnecessary. This plant rarely requires attention and is also trouble-free.

AZARA MICROPHYLLA
The Vanilla tree

This is a beautiful weeping, evergreen tree that has tiny, glossy leaves cascading from its delicate branches. It gets its common name from the incredible vanilla fragrance that oozes from its almost microscopic yellow flowers during early spring.

If left to grow naturally, the plant develops into a large shrub. Removing lower branches as it grows will turn it into a single-stemmed tree – a more shapely option.

KEY FACTS

Min Temp -10°C (14°F)

Soil Light, manure-enriched, free-draining soil

Site Likes light shade, with shelter from strong winds

Vigour Quite slow-growing – even after ten years it is unlikely to exceed 4–5m (13–16½ft)

CARE: Needs constant moisture, particularly during its early growth period. Give an annual dose of blood, fish and bone in spring. Saw off lower branches to create a tree. Pests and diseases do not usually cause any problems.

AZORINA VIDALII

A low-growing, shrubby perennial with long, glossy leaves. Flower spikes appear during summer, opening up into large, waxy, china-pink bells that last for weeks. They have a delicate appearance but, unfortunately, not a delicate fragrance.

Although this plant is not hardy (unless planted in a sheltered inner city or mild coastal garden), because it is evergreen and slow-growing it is an ideal choice for a pot. It can live outside during summer and inside for the chillier months.

KEY FACTS
Min Temp -4°C (24°F)
Soil Any free-draining soil
Site Full sun or partial shade, sheltered from cold winds
Vigour Slow-growing, up to 60cm x 60cm (2ft x 2ft)

CARE: Regular irrigation is required during the growing season; little watering during winter. Give an annual feed of blood, fish and bone in spring. Flower spikes should be cut right down after flowering. Green aphids like the new shoots. During winter, the plant can suffer from grey mould.

BESCHORNERIA YUCCOIDES

This plant is very similar in appearance to some types of yucca but without the spiky bits. It grows huge, clump-forming rosettes of glaucous green leaves. Very little seems to be known about *B. yuccoides* and it is quite rare in cultivation.

The plant's flower spikes are awesome. Massive coral-red stems arch out of the centre of the rosette, followed by numerous rose-red bracts, which in turn develop dozens of nodding green flowers, all of which last for many weeks usually from late spring until midsummer. After flowering, large fig-like (but inedible) fruits appear. Individual rosettes die after flowering, but the plant carries on as normal – eventually forming more and more clumps.

KEY FACTS

Min Temp -10°C (14°F)

Soil Any well-drained soil is suitable, but rich and fertile conditions give the best results

Site Full sun in a sheltered spot away from strong winds

Vigour The rosettes house massive stems, 1.8m (6ft) long. Older plants have several rosettes that reach maturity and flower at the same time

CARE: Once established, irrigation is not necessary unless grown in a pot. Feed in the spring with a mix of blood, fish and bone. When the flowers have finished, cut them off. The rosette that has produced the flowers will die and should then be teased out. Lots more rosettes will grow in its place. Slugs occasionally nibble this plant. If grown in a conservatory, red spider mite can be a regular problem.

BILLBERGIA NUTANS *Queen's tears*

This exotic-looking plant, related to the pineapple, has shiny, strap-like leaves surrounding an urn-shaped centre. Flamingo pink spears emerge from between the foliage and open out into pretty pink and green blossoms.

Choosing the correct site for *B. nutans* can be tricky. In shady, moist positions, the foliage turns a lush deep green, but few flowers are produced. In full sun, the foliage turns a yellowish green, but flowers are produced in abundance. Therefore, something between the two is best.

KEY FACTS

Min Temp -4°C (24°F)
Soil Any free-draining soil, this plant will also grow hanging off trees
Site Light shade
Vigour Clump-forming, can spread to 1m (3ft) across

CARE: Frequent moisture gives the best results. Spray with water weekly if grown indoors. Generally maintenance free, and rarely troubled by pests.

BLECHNUM CHILENSE *Seersucker fern*

This is an absolute monster of a fern. The surface of the fronds is rough to the touch and puckered like seersucker fabric, hence its common name. Ferns can be fussy plants and *B. chilense* is no exception.

KEY FACTS
Min Temp -10°C (14°F)
Soil Light and crumbly – an ideal mix would be equal parts of leaf mould, peat and loam
Site A shady position, sheltered from wind but where air circulation is good. A bank or slope is a good choice as the excess water can then easily drain away
Vigour Can reach more than 1–1.2m (3–4ft)

CARE: Plenty of moisture, but with perfect drainage so that excess water runs away (the plant will not tolerate waterlogging). Does not require feeding. Older brown fronds should be removed. Relatively trouble-free.

BLECHNUM SPICANT

The Hard or deer fern

This evergreen fern has bright emerald fronds fashioned in the shape of a fish skeleton. The fresh growth in the spring is particularly attractive; new fronds uncurl to reveal an even more startling bright green than the adult foliage.

KEY FACTS

Min Temp -20°C (-4°F)
Soil Neutral to acid soil that is light in texture – avoid chalk or lime
Site Happiest in shade; will tolerate some sun. Try to choose a sloping site so that excess water drains away immediately
Vigour Maximum height 45cm (1½ft); clumps spread slowly to 60cm (2ft) across

CARE: Needs moist but not boggy conditions. No annual feeding necessary. Remove older brown fronds as plants age. Pests and diseases not usually a problem.

BRAHEA ARMATA   *Blue hesper palm*

This beautiful desert palm really does have silvery
blue leaves. It is very desirable but unfortunately
tends to survive rather than thrive in outdoor
conditions. The rain, fog and general murk of many
winter climates makes the choice of site difficult.
Being a desert palm, it is more used to crisp dry air –
a different sort of cold altogether. If grown in a mild
climate, plant near to a wall or a house to shield it
from the worst of any wet weather. Otherwise, it is
best grown in a large pot and overwintered indoors
or under glass.

KEY FACTS

Min Temp -4°C (24°F)
Soil Free-draining, gritty soil
is essential for this plant
Site Copes outdoors in full sun
out of strong winds or indoors
in a sunny conservatory
Vigour In the wild, it can
reach up to 12m (40ft) but in
general cultivation is unlikely
to exceed 3m (10ft). It is best to
buy a decent-sized specimen
as it can take 15 years for the
plant to reach 2m (6ft)

CARE: If grown in a pot, water regularly during spring and summer. The plant is drought resistant in the ground. Feed with blood, fish and bone once a year in mid-spring. Remove any older fronds that have turned brown. Red spider mite can be problematic if the plant is grown under glass.

BUTIA CAPITATA

The Jelly palm

This is a fine, stately palm with blue-grey arching leaves. It is surprisingly hardy for such a glamorous-looking tree but needs to be kept fairly dry during the winter, which is often difficult in many climates. If grown in a cold area, it would be better to keep it in a large pot and overwinter indoors or under glass. When the plant and pot become too heavy to move, planting directly into the ground is the only option. In severe winters, the whole plant can be tied up and shrouded in agricultural fleece until spring returns.

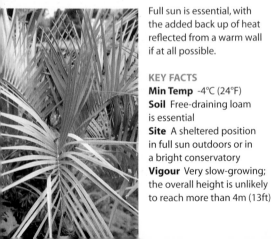

Full sun is essential, with the added back up of heat reflected from a warm wall if at all possible.

KEY FACTS
Min Temp -4°C (24°F)
Soil Free-draining loam is essential
Site A sheltered position in full sun outdoors or in a bright conservatory
Vigour Very slow-growing; the overall height is unlikely to reach more than 4m (13ft)

CARE: Once established, the plant is fairly drought resistant outdoors. Water regularly if in a pot. If grown outside, winter wrapping is necessary. Feed annually in mid-spring by sprinkling a mix of blood, fish and bone around the base. Remove any old and tatty leaves. If grown under glass, watch out for red spider mite and scale insects.

CANNA INDICA *Indian shot plant or canna lily*

This plant is a splendid leafy addition to exotic planting schemes, having large, banana-type leaves and bright yellow and red flowers in summer. The name 'Indian shot plant' refers to the red, which is splattered across the flowers. It is an herbaceous plant, dying back to the rootstock each winter.

Such lilies are traditionally used along the sea fronts in summer bedding displays. Their large leaves seem to cope well with the sea breezes and salty gales. In milder areas, they can be left outside all year. In cold, wet areas, the plants are best dug up in winter and stored in dry peat in a greenhouse. Alternatively, grow them in large pots that can be moved under shelter. Another option is to leave them outside, and mulch heavily with straw or bracken (*see* p. 21).

KEY FACTS

Min Temp -4°C (24°F)

Soil The plant prefers soil that is rich, moist and fertile

Site Ideally full sun, but also gives good results if grown in light shade

Vigour This lily is fast-growing – 1.5m (5ft) of new growth can be produced every year. Plants become bulkier as they age, forming substantial clumps around 1m (3ft) across

CARE: Water a lot during the growing season, allow to dry out during the winter. Add well-rotted manure in late spring. Cut back old leaves. The tender juicy leaves are magnets for every slug in the vicinity.

CANNA IRIDIFLORA   *Giant canna lily*

This plant has a huge mass of giant leaves topped
with the most outrageous, shocking-pink flowers.
It is one of the most essential plants for any garden
with exotic tendencies but, because of its size,
performs less well in windy positions than other
Canna varieties.

Fertile soil, enriched with well-rotted manure, is necessary to get the best from the plant. A sunny spot is preferred, but light shade is acceptable.

In mild gardens, clumps can be left in the ground and mulched with straw or bracken (*see p. 21*). In cold, wet gardens, they are best lifted out of the ground and stored in dry peat in a greenhouse, in much the same way as the more familiar dahlias.

KEY FACTS

Min Temp -4°C (24°F)
Soil Rich, moist and fertile
Site Enjoys sun or light shade, but must be in a sheltered spot
Vigour *Canna iridiflora* can easily reach 2.5m (8ft) in a season before dying back each year, to re-emerge the following spring with even more vigour than it had previously

CARE: Provide copious amounts of water during the growing season, allow to dry out in winter. Add well-rotted manure in late spring. If a specimen produces large quantities of lush green leaves each year, but no flowers, give it tomato food in early summer. This will provide the extra dose of potash required for flower production. Cut back old leaves when frosted. Slugs love this plant.

CARPOBROTUS EDULIS *Hottentot fig*

In mild coastal areas, this succulent ground cover can often be seen cascading down cliffs or scrambling along the edges of beaches. It is exceptionally salt-tolerant and is an essential requirement for any seaside garden. In milder areas, large and often brightly coloured daisy flowers open up during the daytime. In hot summers, these are followed by edible fruits.

KEY FACTS
Min Temp -4°C (24°F)
Soil Will grow in almost any soil
Site Full sun, easily copes with the most exposed, windy sites
Vigour Fast-growing – this plant will spread over enormous distances if it is given the right spot

CARE: In its first season, give the plant regular soakings. Once established, irrigation is unnecessary. Although *C. edulis* will survive on neglect, a light feed at the start of the season gives good results. Nothing seems to bother this tough plant – it can't even be destroyed by fire!

CHAMAEROPS HUMILIS

Dwarf fan palm

This low-growing bushy palm sends up numerous suckers around the base throughout its life, rather than forming a single trunk. The colour of the foliage is very variable, ranging from green, silvery-green to almost blue. During warm summers, after flowering, clusters of large, orange, shiny berries are produced.

C. humilis prefers full sun, although the fronds stay a prettier green if grown in light shade. The foliage is plentiful and the whole clump can become very dense, enabling it to withstand strong winds – making it a brilliantly suitable palm for coastal districts. As this palm is so slow-growing, it is also a reasonably good choice for growing in a pot on a balcony or terrace.

KEY FACTS

Min Temp -10°C (14°F)

Soil *Chamaerops humilis* prefers rich, fertile, well-drained loam, especially when it is being grown out of doors

Site Sun or light shade is tolerated. This plant is an excellent choice for growing in very exposed positions

Vigour The plant is slow-growing and its height at maturity is realistically only around 2m (6½ft)

CARE: Drought tolerant once established, water moderately when in growth. Feed with a mix of blood, fish and bone in spring and early summer. Remove all brown leaves as they appear. Brown leaf spot is common. Under glass, red spider mite can be a problem.

CLEMATIS ARMANDII

This large-leafed, evergreen climber can grow just about anywhere. It is not self-clinging, but can quickly wind itself around drainpipes and trellis or up through trees. The flowers are borne throughout spring, and will even appear as early as late winter if the weather has been mild. They are pure white and very lightly fragrant.

KEY FACTS

Min Temp -20°C (-4°F)
Soil Well-drained alkaline soil is preferred, but the plant will grow in any soil
Site Sun or shade in a sheltered position – the more sun, the more flowers it will produce
Vigour The plant is very vigorous, easily reaching 6m (20ft)

CARE: Water the plant regularly for the first couple of seasons until it is established. Give a light sprinkling of blood, fish and bone mix in late spring. Check for whitefly if buying a plant that has been grown under glass.

COLLETIA CRUCIATA
(syn. *Colletia paradoxa*)

This extremely unusual plant has vicious leaves,
which are actually modified branches, borne in pairs
and set at right angles to the ones directly beneath.
They are flat, fleshy and triangular with each one
ending in a sharp tip. The flowers are a calm contrast
to the foliage. They are dainty little bells of the very
palest cream that waft the delicious scent of almonds
around the garden for many months from the end of
summer until early spring. Butterflies and bees enjoy
this plant immensely.

If forced to grow in a pot, the plant is very unhappy
and can stay the same size for years, absolutely
refusing to grow at all. For propagation purposes,
semi-ripe cuttings planted into the soil is the best
method to reproduce from this plant.

KEY FACTS

Min Temp -10°C (14°F)

Soil Any soil type, preferably moderately fertile, as long as it is well-drained

Site Full sun is ideal for this plant – it is excellent for exposed gardens

Vigour Growth is fairly slow, but can reach a height and spread of 2.5m (8ft) in ten years

CARE: If planted into the ground watering is rarely required, especially during winter. The plant is virtually maintenance free but it can thrive with an annual feed of a blood, fish and bone mix. *Colletia cruciata* is refreshingly free from blight by pests and diseases.

CORDYLINE AUSTRALIS   *Cabbage palm*

This plant is a fine example of exotica, despite being neither a cabbage nor a palm, as its common name suggests. Corky trunks are topped with a bushy head of long, narrow leaves that are very tolerant of salty winds, making it an excellent choice for a seaside garden. The flowers are large, white clusters that smell absolutely exquisite – the fragrance can waft across the air and be detected from considerable distances away. After flowering, the head of foliage will divide into two or three branches, eventually building up into huge masses.

C. australis is commonly seen growing in pots as part of a summer bedding scheme. They are suitable for pots for one season only and should then be planted into the ground.

KEY FACTS

Min Temp -4°C (24°F)
Soil Good-quality loam is preferred, but generally not too fussy
Site Sun or light shade. This is a good tree for planting in exposed, windy gardens
Vigour A fast-growing tree that can reach 5–6m (16½–20ft) and be grown as either single- or multi-stemmed

CARE: Good drainage is essential as too much moisture will rot the roots, causing collapse. Regular brown-bitting is required to keep it looking cared for (*see* pp 22–23). Winter wrapping from mid-winter until early spring should be considered (*see* p. 21). *Cordyline australis* is usually fairly trouble-free outside but red spider mite is a frequent pest on specimens grown in conservatories.

CROCOSMIA 'LUCIFER'   *Montbretia*

The fiery scarlet flowers are the main appeal of this plant. They are not just vividly coloured but are also produced in copious amounts. They are grown from corms and die back each autumn. Growth starts again during mid- to late spring, sending up lots of grassy leaves that open out into narrow sword shapes.

These plants are best grown in large drifts to give a dramatic effect. They bulk up quickly and can spread over fairly wide areas. A small woodland garden

would be perfect where they can naturalise without being curbed. If they outgrow their allocated space in the garden, simply dig up chunks with a spade and dispose of them or replant them elsewhere. In exceptionally cold gardens, the bulbs are best lifted and stored for the duration of the winter in trays of fairly dry peat under a greenhouse bench.

KEY FACTS

Min Temp -20°C (-4°F)

Soil Prefers to grow in light, moderately fertile soil that is free-draining

Site Full sun or light shade, ideally sheltered from strong winds

Vigour Quick-growing, the foliage can be up to 1m (3ft) tall with the flower spikes adding another 60cm (2ft)

CARE: Keep moist during the growing season, but the soil should never become boggy. Feed in spring with well-rotted manure. In autumn, after the foliage has turned brown, cut back hard to ground level. Pests and diseases do not usually cause any problems.

CYNARA CARDUNCULUS *Cardoon*

This is a huge brute of a plant. Its leaves are deeply cut, soft to the touch, pale greenish-grey in colour and achieve enormous dimensions.

The plant is perfect for the back of planting schemes. Rising above the foliage in mid- to late summer, flower stems become visible. The flower heads start off looking like mini artichokes, then open up into large thistles. These are actually electric blue but photographs (as you can see!) never do justice to this colour so try and see some in the flesh.

KEY FACTS

Min Temp -20°C (-4°F)

Soil The plant must be put into very rich and fertile soil in order to achieve its maximum growth

Site Full sun is preferred in a sheltered spot, protected from strong winds

Vigour *Cynara cardunculus* grows with phenomenal speed – after its dormant period, an established plant that has been overwintered in the ground can quite easily grow to be 2.5m (8ft) high and over 2m (6ft) wide during just a single growing season

CARE: Lots of water is required during the growing season, but the soil around the plant must not become boggy. Feed it heavily in mid-spring with lots of well-rotted manure or several handfuls of blood, fish and bone. Cut tired and yellow leaves down to the ground in winter. This plant is adored by slugs and snails.

CYPERUS ALTERNIFOLIUS
Dwarf papyrus or umbrella plant

This is a pretty little perennial grass like a miniature papyrus, only much tougher. It can be grown outside throughout the year in mild inner city gardens and most coastal areas. If outside, either grow it in a pond or a very boggy site where it has permanent access to water. It will die down each year and send up new shoots in spring. This plant can also be grown quite successfully indoors in the conservatory, where it remains evergreen.

Although there are the usual methods of propagation – such as using division or else by fresh seed – you can also chop off one of the heads from the plant with a long piece of stalk attached, turn it upside down and push it into a glass container filled with water. Roots will form from what was previously the top and new shoots will start to grow from the centre. When a manageable-sized plant has developed, pot it up.

KEY FACTS
Min Temp -4°C (24°F)
Soil Unfussy but needs moisture in the soil
Site Full sun or light shade in a sheltered spot
Vigour Forms clumps of long, bright green stalks that can reach 1m (3ft) tall

CARE: This plant must never be allowed to dry out – it is impossible to overwater. Chop off old leaves at the base when they become untidy. Fairly trouble-free but look out for aphids on new growth during spring and early summer.

DANAE RACEMOSA   *Alexandrian laurel*

This plant is somewhere between a miniature bamboo and a bunch of asparagus. The new shoots are the start of its 'asparagus' phase, poking up in mid- to late spring. As the plant matures, larger clumps of it begin to form, hence its 'bamboo' phase. After a very warm summer, bright red berries appear.

This plant is useful for places in the garden where little else will grow – you could try, for example, growing it beneath an evergreen tree.

KEY FACTS
Min Temp -20°C (-4°F)
Soil Rich soil preferred; can cope with poorer conditions
Site Light shade, but deep shade acceptable
Vigour Very slow to spread; it will grow about 1m (3ft) in ten years

CARE: Regular irrigation best, but dry positions are tolerated. The plant is generally maintenance free, although old shoots can be cut back to ground level in the spring. If confined to a pot, vine weevil are virtually guaranteed.

DAPHNE ODORA 'AUREOMARGINATA'

A small, evergreen plant with shiny foliage that forms a rounded dome made up of fresh green leaves. These leaves are subtly edged with pale cream variegation. Flowers open up from mid-winter until early spring when there is very little else in flower in the rest of the garden. The only slight drawback is that the plant can be a bit short-lived.

KEY FACTS

Min Temp -20°C (-4°F)
Soil Flourishes best in neutral to alkaline soil that is well-drained
Site Full sun or light shade. Choose position carefully as replanting may kill it
Vigour It is rare to see a clump bigger than 1.2m (4ft) across

CARE: Soil should be kept moist but not boggy. Give a light feed with a handful of blood, fish and bone in late spring. Green aphids like the new growing tips of this plant.

DASYLIRION ACROTRICHUM
Green desert spoon

This is an incredible plant. From the centre of each rosette emerge hundreds of very thin, serrated leaves all of which are tipped with a feathery tuft. As more and more leaves develop, the older ones are pushed down until an almost perfect sphere is built up. After many years, as the older leaves are removed, a little stubby trunk starts to form. Absurd-looking flower spikes are occasionally sent out from the centre. Spectacular as they are, they spoil the symmetry of the plant so simply chop them off.

Dasylirion is the ultimate landscape plant as it can be appreciated from a distance. For this reason, plant it so it has plenty of space around it. It is practically hurricane-proof and can shrug off even the most severe salty gales, so is a great choice for the coast. It can also be grown in a large terracotta container.

KEY FACTS
Min Temp -10°C (14°F)
Soil Any that is sharply drained. Extra grit in the planting hole is beneficial
Site Full sun – excellent for slopes or windy gardens
Vigour Slow-growing – can reach 1.5m (5ft) in diameter in 30 years

Care: Watering is unnecessary unless grown in a pot. Sprinkle a couple of handfuls of blood, fish and bone around the base of mature plants in late spring. Pests and diseases do not usually cause any problems.

DICKSONIA ANTARCTICA

*Tasmanian
tree fern*

This amazing fern is one of the world's most beautiful
plants. A thick, fibrous, chocolate-brown trunk is
topped with huge, deeply cut fronds 2m (6½ft) long.
It starts to form a trunk after five years.

This fern is extremely fussy in its requirements –
it is almost like buying a pet. Shade is essential, so
is a sheltered position. Humidity is very important
and mild gardens are necessary to keep it outside
all-year-round. Otherwise, keep it in a very large
pot and overwinter in a shady, cool conservatory.
Alternatively, follow the winter wrapping method
using straw bales (*see* p. 21).

KEY FACTS

Min Temp -4°C (24°F)
Soil Peat mixed with leaf mould and silver sand
to help with the drainage would be ideal
Site Shade and shelter from wind. Avoid planting
where people can brush against it
Vigour *Dicksonia antarctica* grows at a rate of
only 30cm (1ft) every ten years, so buying a baby
plant will need a lot of time and patience to see
it develop into something spectacular.

CARE: Needs regular irrigation throughout the growing
season – ideally the trunk should be sprayed twice daily
during the hot summer months. Apply liquid feed every
month from spring until midsummer. Wrap up in winter
(*see* p. 21). If fronds go brown cut off at the base. Pests and
diseases do not usually cause any problems.

ECHEVERIA GLAUCA

A delightful, clump-forming succulent that has pale blue fleshy leaves. In the summer, a flower spike emerges from each clump, with several bell-shaped red flowers with yellow tips.

A popular addition to summer bedding schemes, the plant can stay outside all year in mild gardens. It is excellent in gravel gardens and a superb choice for a terracotta pot. It can also be used to liven up rockeries. If placed in borders, the plant looks more effective planted in large groups.

KEY FACTS
Min Temp -4°C (24°F)
Soil Any: add extra grit
Site Enjoys full sun – copes with exposed coastal gardens
Vigour Slow-growing; individual rosettes reach 15cm (6in) across

CARE: Water sparingly in summer, not at all in winter. No feeding necessary. Remove old leaves or flower stems. Slugs like this plant – if grown in a pot, watch out for vine weevil.

ECHIUM PININANA

Tree echium

This plant reigns supreme as King of all the exotics. If your garden is a mild one, then this woody herb is unquestionably essential. The plant has a life cycle that spreads over two years, starting with the planting of small seedlings in early spring.

Take care when handling the plant – always wear gloves – it is densely covered with bristles that rub off easily, causing an itchy rash if they get under the skin. Getting it through the first winter is the real challenge. It is difficult to wrap up and protect from frost.

After the winter, growth starts again in early spring. With surprising rapidity the stem starts to get longer and the new

foliage becomes smaller and smaller as the stem extends and romps away into the air. The flower buds grow to cover the entire top half of the stem. The flowers then open out into hundreds of purplish-blue blossoms and are sheer heaven to bees. Flowers last for many weeks but then the plant dies. One compensation, however, is that many seeds will probably be scattered all around the garden.

KEY FACTS

Min Temp -4°C (24°F)
Soil Any, but good-quality, well-drained soil preferred
Site Full sun or light shade. The plant thrives in mild, coastal gardens
Vigour Fast-growing – seedlings grow to 1.2–1.5m (4–5ft) in the first growing season. The flower stem eventually reaches 4m (13ft)

CARE: Water only when newly planted. After this, the plant takes care of itself. Protect from frost during winter. Pests and diseases do not usually cause problems.

ERYNGIUM AGAVIFOLIUM

A spiny perennial plant with wide, bright emerald leaves. These are edged with hooked barbs that look more ferocious than they actually are. Flower spikes are sent up during early summer and look like large greenish-yellow thimbles on short stalks. Although not beautiful they do attract bees.

E. agavifolium is easy to cultivate and looks better planted in groups of at least three plants. They are ideal for the front of borders, in rockeries or planted in gravel gardens. They are not suitable for growing in pots.

KEY FACTS
Min Temp -20°C (-4°F)
Soil Light, sandy, free-draining soil
Site Full sun
Vigour Height and spread rarely more than 60cm (2ft)

CARE: Water frequently until established. In a harsh winter, foliage can become tatty. The whole plant should then be cut back to ground level with a sharp knife. Slugs can be a nuisance, and green aphids like the new shoots.

EUCALYPTUS AGGREGATA   *The Black gum*

This is the perfect tree to form a screen. Its leaves are long, narrow and glaucous-green and, when crushed, emit the familiar aromatic eucalyptus scent.

E. aggregata grows naturally as a multi-stemmed tree, which is not practical for smaller gardens. Instead, train it as a single-stemmed specimen by removing lower branches gradually, until all branches and foliage are above head height. This ensures that

the only space taken up in the garden is the diameter of the trunk.

KEY FACTS

Min Temp -20°C (-4°F)

Soil Poor, neutral to acid soil preferred, although some lime or chalk is acceptable

Site Sunny but sheltered spot. Windy, exposed sites tolerated if heavily staked

Vigour Extremely fast-growing; can easily reach 9m (30ft) in six years

CARE: Almost impossible to overwater. Can also cope with near-drought conditions. Virtually maintenance free. Usually untroubled by pests and diseases.

EUCALYPTUS NIPHOPHILA
'DEBEUZEVILLEI'

Jounama snow gum

There are several different snow gums, but the variety 'Debeuzevillei' is one of the most wonderful. The bark on the trunk and along the branches is a beautiful mixture of different-coloured patches ranging from snowy white, pale grey, silvery grey, cream and palest beige. The tree's leaves are large, leathery, blue-grey and also highly aromatic.

This tree is much smaller than many of the other hardy gum trees, making it the best variety of eucalyptus for growing in small gardens. It can be left as a large multi-stemmed bush, but it is also perfectly suitable for training as a single-stemmed tree simply by removing all the lower branches as required. When newly planted, stakes are a good option to support fast-growing foliage. This plant is an excellent choice as a specimen feature if there is only room in the garden for one special evergreen tree.

KEY FACTS

Min Temp -20°C (-4°F)
Soil Sandy, well-drained, neutral to acid soil is best. Must be lime-free
Site Full sun in a sheltered position away from any strong winds
Vigour Slow-growing – takes at least ten years to reach its maximum height of 8m (25ft)

CARE: Watering is only necessary for newly planted trees, as too much water can damage the roots. The plant is more or less maintenance free. This variety usually has few problems with pests and diseases.

EUPHORBIA MELLIFERA *Honey spurge*

The common name of 'honey spurge' refers to the flowers, which are not only honey coloured but have the same delicious smell, too. They appear in liberal quantities during late spring.

E. mellifera is hopeless in a pot, so plant it out. Wear gloves whenever cutting into it, as the milky white sap exuded from the cut stems and leaves of all euphorbias can be an irritant to eyes and skin.

KEY FACTS
Min Temp -10°C (14°F)
Soil Prefers a rich, fertile soil
Site Sun or light shade in a sheltered spot – try to give it the warmest site in the garden
Vigour Fast-growing; can reach a height and spread of 2m (6½ft) high within three years

CARE: Water well to start with – once established this is unnecessary. Cut back to the base if it becomes too 'leggy'. Check for capsid bug and aphids. If the plant is grown under glass, whitefly and red spider mite are troublesome.

EUPHORBIA MYRSINITES

Creeping spurge

Easy to cultivate, *E. myrsinites* is the perfect ground cover to complement spiky plants such as yuccas and agaves. It adores full sun and drapes itself all around the base of every plant it encounters, providing a thick undercover.

The plant's long, fleshy runners are edged with blue leaves, which are small and attractively shaped into a point. They look succulent like those of a desert plant but, when inspected more closely, are in fact quite flat. The flowers (which are really protuberances called bracts) are bright greenish-yellow and appear during early spring. Inside each one is the true flower, which is a tiny yellow dot.

This plant remains evergreen and is totally hardy. It is easy to cultivate but make sure you wear gloves when cutting into it, due to its skin-irritating sap.

KEY FACTS
Min Temp -20°C (-4°F)
Soil Grows in any soil as long as it is well-drained
Site Full sun is an essential requirement
Vigour *Euphorbia myrsinites* can cover an area of around ¹/₂ sq m (2sq ft) in two years

CARE: Water *E. myrsinites* when it is first planted, but, after that, you can ignore it except during long, dry periods. No feeding required. After flowering, cut off the dead flower spikes back to the leafy parts of each stem. Older plants can also become straggly, which can be solved by pruning back fairly hard. This encourages new growth to sprout from the central rosette. Pests and diseases do not usually cause this plant any problems.

EUPHORBIA WULFENII   *Spurge*

This is a versatile plant that can be successfully incorporated into most planting schemes. It can look just as good with spiky plants as it does in a shrubby or flowery border. It looks rather fetching in gravel gardens, where the colour of the leaves can be shown off to good effect. In spacious gardens, *E. wulfenii* looks wonderful if planted in large groups. It also grows well in coastal gardens; the salty winds do not seem to affect it. The plant's foliage is a dark, steely blue and produced in abundance. The showy flower heads are made up of startling sulphur yellow bracts, surrounding a tiny yellow dot that is the real flower. They last for many weeks from early to late spring.

Propagation is easy from seed – buy this from a reputable seed company instead of collecting it yourself. These plants hybridise easily and can produce very variable adult plants. As with all euphorbias, take care of the milky sap that oozes from the stem when it is cut.

CARE: Drought tolerant once established. Remove old flower heads when they turn brown. If the plant becomes too leggy, prune it back to the base. It is rarely bothered by pests and diseases.

KEY FACTS

Min Temp -20°C (-4°F)

Soil Fertile soil is preferred, but it will cope with poor chalky conditions. Must be well-drained

Site Full sun or light shade. Grows particularly well in coastal gardens

Vigour Can reach 1.2m (4ft) tall and the same in width within five years

FASCICULARIA BICOLOR   *Firewheel*

This is the hardiest member of the *Bromeliaceae* family, which means it is closely related to the pineapple. It is made up of tightly packed bundles of narrow, prickly leaves. These mass together forming individual rosettes that pile up on each other, gradually creating huge clumps of impenetrable foliage. They either spread sideways across the ground or hang down over stone walls. They can even be persuaded to climb up fibrous tree trunks.

During the summer, the centre of mature rosettes produce astonishing vivid scarlet inner leaves circling a centre of bright turquoise blue flowers.

If the plant is grown in the ground, a sloping site is preferred so that any excess water drains away. It is a perfect choice for planting in a stone trough, for hanging over walls and growing on rockeries. It can even be tied into trees where it is quite happy growing as an epiphyte.

CARE: Water infrequently. The plant takes care of itself once established. No maintenance required, except cutting out old rosettes that are scruffy. Pests and diseases rarely a problem, although dead flower heads can attract woodlice.

KEY FACTS

Min Temp -10℃ (14°F)

Soil Free-draining gritty soil. If the plant is in a pot, use John Innes No. 3 with extra grit stirred in

Site Full sun or light shade – it can also cope well in exposed conditions

Vigour The plant grows to a maximum of 45cm (1½ft) with a spread of 60cm (2ft)

FATSHEDERA LIZEI   *Fat-headed Lizzie*

A large-leafed, evergreen jungly climber that can either climb up trellis or be left to scramble across the ground. It is a cross between *Hedera helix* 'Hibernica', which provides its robust qualities, and *Fatsia japonica* 'Moseri', from which it inherits its good looks.

The odd-looking cream-coloured flower spikes produced in the autumn are not things of great beauty, so remove them if you wish. This will ensure all the plant's energy goes into leaf production.

KEY FACTS
Min Temp -20°C (-4°F)
Soil Rich, fertile and well-drained moist soil – neutral to acid preferred
Site Full shade with at least some shelter
Vigour Grows quickly

CARE: Moist conditions or regular watering is required for this climber. Feed the plant regularly during its growing season with a high nitrogen content food. Remove any brown/yellow leaves. Black aphids can be a problem on the new shoots in early summer.

FATSIA JAPONICA

Fig-leafed palm or false castor oil plant

As *F. japonica* is sometimes sold as a houseplant, it is often assumed that it is not hardy enough for the garden. However, it is a fantastic addition to a jungly garden and can cope brilliantly with deep shade.

This is a perfect plant for filling a large, shady corner. In late summer, cream-coloured flower spikes rise up from the centre, which can be removed. If they are left on, bunches of tiny inedible black fruits appear when the flowers have finished.

KEY FACTS

Min Temp - 20°C (-4°F)
Soil Rich, fertile soil preferred
Site Shade
Vigour Slow-growing, although mature plants can reach 2.5m (8ft) tall and 2m (6½ft) wide

CARE: Plenty of moisture required. Feed heavily mid-spring with blood, fish and bone sprinkled around the base. Remove older, yellow leaves. Black aphids are often found on new shoots; capsid bug can spoil the large leaves.

FICUS CARICA

The Common fig

Rarely grown for its superb architectural qualities, *Ficus carica* actually blends in beautifully with exotic planting schemes if it is grown as a proper (albeit deciduous) tree. The plant has lovely silvery-grey bark, topped with copious amounts of enormous, lobed leaves. On hot sunny days, the leaves can give off a very pleasant aroma.

Unless grown under glass or in a mild garden, the fruit can often be an unrewarding experience, so the instructions given below help produce a fine-looking foliage plant.

KEY FACTS
Min Temp -20°C (-4°F)
Soil Rich, moist and fertile conditions
Site A sheltered spot in the shade – the more shade, the bigger the leaves
Vigour Slow-growing – unlikely to exceed 5m (16½ft) in height

CARE: Water regularly – the plant prefers moist, but never boggy, conditions. Prune it back hard each year when dormant. Capsid bug can disfigure the leaves. Coral spot is sometimes a problem on older plants.

FREMONTODENDRON 'CALIFORNIA GLORY'

Flannel bush

Although not desperately architectural or particularly noticeable in the winter, there is one excellent reason for having this plant in the garden – the flowers. They are bright yellow, produced in copious amounts and last for many weeks during early summer.

This plant is a bit of a fusspot and can take a while to get going. Choose the planting site carefully as, once planted, it resents any root disturbance. It can also be somewhat short-lived, but the flowers more than make up for this.

KEY FACTS

Min Temp -10°C (14°F)
Soil Poor and well-drained. Especially good for chalky or sandy soils
Site Full sun, by a sun-baked wall
Vigour Reaches 5m (16½ft) in five years

CARE: Water frequently until established; it is then drought tolerant. No feeding required. Rarely needs pruning but, if necessary, do so immediately after flowering. Not usually prone to any ailments or pests.

GUNNERA MANICATA   *Giant rhubarb*

This is definitely not a plant for the timid gardener. With almost no care at all, *G. manicata* can be big; with proper care and attention this plant can be an absolute monster. It has enormous leaves and huge, dark pink flower spikes are often thrown up from the middle of the plant.

The stems and leaves all grow from a central crown that gets bigger and bulkier each year. This is the delicate part of the plant and can need some protection during the winter, especially in its earlier years. As the leaves die back each year, fold the brown

frosted foliage over the crown to give it some useful on-site protection. This can be left on all winter until the following spring. The previous year's foliage can then either be disposed of or trodden in around the plant to provide extra nutrients as they rot down.

G. manicata is suitable for any boggy area where the roots have unlimited access to plenty of water. Do not permanently submerge them in water though.

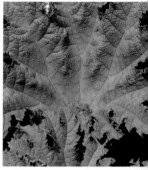

KEY FACTS
Min Temp -20°C (-4°F)
Soil Is unfussy, but does prefer rich, moist and fertile conditions
Site Sun or shade in a sheltered spot
Vigour This is a very large plant – individual leaves often reach over 45cm (1½ft) across

Care: A regular supply of water is required throughout the plant's life. Removing the flower spikes before they open will put all the plant's energy into making bigger leaves. Pests and diseases do not usually cause any problems.

HEBE PARVIFLORA ANGUSTIFOLIA

'A giant, evergreen cushion' sums up this plant in a nutshell. It is a round, soft-looking plant with long narrow leaves, which stay emerald green all-year-round, but is immensely tough. It can be grown in a wide range of conditions but is particularly useful for dry shade where very little else will grow. It looks a bit like a miniature willow, with the added bonus of being evergreen. Because the foliage is so dense, the plant also makes a perfect hedge, which gets thicker the more it is clipped. Fuzzy grey-white flowers are produced in early summer – they do nothing to enhance the plant and can be removed.

The only place where this plant will not thrive is crammed into a small pot. Planting directly into the ground is essential. It is very easy to cultivate and fits into most planting schemes, being especially useful for planting beneath trees.

KEY FACTS
Min Temp -20°C (-4°F)
Soil Any, as long as it is in the ground
Site Sun or shade, although protection from cold winds is desirable
Vigour Fast-growing – this plant can easily reach 2m (6½ft) tall and wide in five years

Care: Will cope with either being well-watered or ignored. If grown as a hedge, clip little and often from mid-spring to late summer – don't cut into old wood. Generally trouble-free from pests and diseases, unless confined to a pot.

HEDYCHIUM COCCINEUM 'TARA'

Tara's ginger lily

This tropical-looking perennial gets bigger and better with age. The large, pointed leaves surround a thick fleshy stem. The flowers are an unusual deep orange and last for many weeks. The flower head is made up of dozens of individual blooms massed together in a cylindrical shape at the end of each stem. Bees adore them. The plants grow in clumps that are best planted in groups of at least three. Flowering starts after three years, and the number of flower stems increases each year.

Once planted, *Hedychium coccineum* 'Tara' is best left undisturbed. The life cycle of this plant starts in spring, when rhizomes are planted outside during late spring. They perform much better if they are planted directly into the ground, but a large container is an acceptable option.

Care: Water the plant a lot during its growing season. During winter, tip pots up to let water drain out of them. Very greedy, this plant will consume whatever food it is given. In colder areas, mulch the ground with straw in winter for extra root protection (*see* p. 21). Outdoors, usually trouble-free. In a conservatory, red spider mite could be a problem.

Towards the end of summer, the flower stems will have reached their maximum height and odd lumpy-looking things will start to protrude. These will open up into flowers, which will be in their full glory between early and mid-autumn. After this, the foliage will gradually turn yellow and die back.

KEY FACTS

Min Temp -10°C (14°F)

Soil Rich, loamy and fertile. Well-drained conditions are vital for this plant

Site Prefers full sun or light shade in a sheltered spot

Vigour *Hedychium coccineum* 'Tara' spreads slowly – a trio of clumps planted next to each other will cover just 1sq m (about 1sq yd) after five years

HEDYCHIUM FORRESTII   *Ginger lily*

This is not only one of the tallest ginger lilies but also one of the hardiest, suitable for most climates except for very cold, wet gardens. The leaves are dark green, large and pointed. The flowers are pure white and massed together to form a cylindrical shape. They are popular with bees. Too tall to keep confined to a pot, this plant should be planted outside in groups directly into the soil. Choose the planting position carefully as it prefers to be left undisturbed.

The flowering season is from late summer until mid-autumn. After this, the foliage starts to turn yellow and die down for the winter. The plant is slow to regrow the following year, but, once started, growth is rapid. The typical lumpy growths that emerge from the stems and open up into flowers become noticeable during late summer.

KEY FACTS
Min Temp -10°C (14°F)
Soil Rich, loamy, fertile and well-drained
Site Full sun or light shade in a sheltered spot
Vigour Slow to spread out, it can take years to fill a decent-sized space. However, the plant quickly grows back up each year until the flower stems reach a height of 2m (6½ft)

Care: Masses of water is required during the growing season but this must not collect around the roots. Cut off old foliage when yellow and unsightly. Feed this plant with generous amounts of well-rotted manure. Pests and diseases do not usually cause any problems.

HELLEBORUS FOETIDUS   *Stinking hellebore*

If your garden is shady and the soil is chalky, this evergreen plant is the perfect choice and should be planted in copious amounts. The leaves are finely cut, dark green and glossy. Flowers are lime green and the flowering period lasts for several months, usually from early winter to mid-spring.

Once plants are settled in, seeds are regularly produced and scattered all over the garden, so that small seedlings can be found filling any spare space they find. They are easily removed and not invasive enough to become a nuisance.

Despite its common name, there is absolutely nothing unpleasant about the smell of the leaves or flowers. *Helleborus foetidus* can be planted in large drifts in shady borders or in groups underneath trees. They are also tolerant of seaside gardens and do not seem to mind being on the receiving end of the occasional blast of salty air.

KEY FACTS

Min Temp -20°C (-4°F)

Soil Any – excellent in chalk, but fertile, well-drained loam is the favourite choice

Site Grows well in light to deep shade in either a sheltered or exposed position

Vigour Small plants grow rapidly to 60cm (2ft) and then stop, but each year the flower heads get larger. Mature flower stems can be smothered with over 150 flowers

Care: This plant prefers to be kept moist, but tolerates dry conditions well. If the soil is poor, a light feed of blood, fish and bone can be sprinkled around the base during the growing season. Check regularly for green aphids.

HOLBOELLIA LATIFOLIA

A wonderful evergreen climber blessed with many virtues. Foliage is a very dense mass of fresh green, slightly leathery leaves that lay flat to a wall or fence. Stems can twine around wires or trellis quite easily if given a bit of coaxing in the right direction.

The fragrance from this plant's flowers is so strong that an entire garden can be filled with exquisite scent with just one plant. The flowers are either pale greenish-white if male and tinged pink if female – both smell delicious. They last about six to eight weeks during spring. On mature plants, or after a very warm summer, peculiar-looking fruits appear during early autumn. These start off pale green but gradually enlarge until they are 10cm (4in) long, then they ripen into a bright pinkish-purple colour in mid-autumn. Although edible, they taste rather unexciting so are best left on the plant.

The plant is usually sold with a bamboo cane support in its pot – leave this on and after a couple of seasons it will soon be concealed.

KEY FACTS
Min Temp -10°C (14°F)
Soil Any but prefers well-drained soil that is rich, moist and fertile
Site Sun or shade, can cope with quite windy sites reasonably well
Vigour Growth is very vigorous, once the roots have settled in, and can cover an average-sized fence panel in three years

Care: Fairly drought resistant once it has become properly established. Appreciates very generous amounts of well-rotted manure annually in spring. Prune as necessary at any time of year. Aphids can be a problem on new shoots but generally trouble-free from other pests and mites.

IRIS CONFUSA

The Confused iris

This particular plant is fully deserving of its common name, 'confused iris', because it gives the distinct impression of not quite being able to make up its mind what it is. It does not look or behave as most irises would, but has characteristic traits of both bamboo and palm trees. The stems are definitely reminiscent of a bamboo, being quite hard and woody. These are topped by what looks like a type of palm leaf with fronds made up of individual 'fingers' that are broad and flat.

The flowers are of secondary interest, but are delicate and quite pleasing to the eye. They are long-lasting and appear during mid- to late spring. White, they are tinged slightly with mauve and the occasional yellow mark along the petals.

The plant thrives if it is planted at the base of a sun-baked wall, so that extra heat is reflected from the bricks behind. The soil at the base of such walls also tends to be drier, which suits it admirably. The plant also does quite well if it is grown in a pot, provided the container is at least 45cm (1½ft) across – preferably bigger.

KEY FACTS

Min Temp -10°C (14°F)

Soil Any that is fertile and thoroughly well-drained

Site Full sun in a sheltered spot. Light shade tends to produce fewer flowers

Vigour The stems grow to around 60cm (2ft) in height, and are topped by leaves with fronds 20cm (8in) across

CARE: Happy in dryish conditions unless grown in a pot, where it will need regular irrigation. Feeding is not usually necessary. Remove yellowing leaves, cutting them off as near to the base as possible. The plant is a magnet for slugs.

KNIPHOFIA CAULESCENS/NORTHIAE
Red hot poker

Kniphofia caulescens

There are many different types of kniphofia available and all of them seem to share the same common name of red hot poker, which describes the flowers beautifully. Many kniphofias are grown for their flowers alone, but, occasionally, the foliage is special enough to be the main attraction. *K. caulescens* is certainly in this category. Lovely rosettes of blue-grey foliage give it the kind of tropical appearance that some of the yuccas have, but without the sharp bits. *Kniphofia northiae* is the biggest and chunkiest kniphofia of all.

These lovely South African beasts fit beautifully into any architectural garden, whether it is jungly, spiky or flowery. They look wonderful in gravel gardens and can also be kept in pots for several years.

Propagation can be done by division, but is slow, so growing from fresh seed is the best option.

KEY FACTS

Min Temp -20°C (-4°F)

Soil Rich, fertile and free-draining

Site Full sun – *K. northiae* also likes shelter

Vigour *K. caulescens* slowly grows into clumps, which throw up woody stems from their centres, while *K. northiae* grows a solitary specimen up to 1m (3ft) tall

CARE: *K. northiae* is a greedy plant needing lots of food and water, while *K. caulescens* becomes drought resistant once established. Both appreciate large dollops of well-rotted manure applied annually during late spring. Beware – slugs love these plants and snails will chomp on *K. caulescens*.

Kniphofia northiae

LAMPRANTHUS SPECTABILIS
Hardy mesembryanthemum

This is a hardy succulent that grows thickly to provide a dense matt, which is the perfect foil for all larger spiky plants. It complements agaves, dasylirions and yuccas brilliantly, making it excellent undergrowth for desert gardens. It also looks perfectly at home when it is used as under-planting in Mediterranean-style gardens, contrasting particularly well with palms. This plant can be used to cover sloping banks and rockeries or can be left to cascade down over walls and the edges of big stone troughs. The large, daisy-like magenta flowers open up during the summer when the weather is sunny.

Ends taken from mature plants can be used for propagation – alternatively, *L. spectabilis* can easily be raised from fresh seed.

Care: Water in new plants for first few weeks. Very drought resistant once established. Give a light feed with a small amount of blood, fish and bone in late spring or early summer. As a precaution, hose down the plant and water in the food immediately to prevent scorching. Mature plants can become straggly, so trim back the ends to encourage new, bushier tips. This plant is usually pest- and disease-free.

KEY FACTS

Min Temp -10°C (14°F)

Soil Any that is gritty and well-drained

Site Full sun – the plant copes well with exposed coastal conditions

Vigour Fast-growing – roughly 30sq cm (1sq ft) can increase tenfold with ease after two years of planting

LIBERTIA FORMOSA

A gentle, well-behaved perennial with tufts of grassy leaves that emerge from a central clump. These flat, evergreen leaves are sent up in numerous quantities, making the plant more substantial with each growing season. The whole plant has the appearance of a miniature phormium. Tall flower spikes emerge from the centre during mid-spring and are usually fully open by late spring. Each spike consists of wiry stems that are adorned with many clusters of orchid-like tri-petalled flowers, which are bright white with yellow stamens. These last for many weeks.

Although much better-quality plants are always produced if they are planted directly into the ground, *Libertia formosa* will still provide pleasing results if it is confined to a terracotta pot. It can actually remain relatively content in a container for several years.

KEY FACTS

Min Temp -10°C (14°F)

Soil The plant will grow anywhere, but light, loamy soil is preferred – John Innes No. 3 if in a pot

Site Full sun to light shade, but likes a sheltered position

Vigour A mature plant can be nearly 1m (3ft) across and will produce 30–40 flower stems a year

Care: Once established, very little irrigation is required. If growing in a pot, regular watering will be needed. An annual feed with blood, fish and bone in spring would be beneficial. Remove any older, yellow-brown leaves. Pests are rarely a problem, but check for the occasional aphid on the ends of the flower buds.

LIGUSTRUM LUCIDUM   *Chinese cloud tree*

This is a fantastic evergreen tree from China with a shapely, rounded head, hence the common name of 'Cloud tree'. Left to its own devices, it can grow as a large shrub, but it is much more handsome if grown as a tree. Leaves are large and glossy and masses of frothy, fragrant white flowers are produced in late summer, followed by clusters of blue-black fruits in late autumn. Its wind tolerance is surprisingly good for a large-leafed tree.

Ligustrum lucidum needs plenty of space around it so that its architectural shape can be fully appreciated. It is a very easy tree to grow, requiring virtually no maintenance. When first planted, some initial support

will be needed and a strong tree stake should be used for at least two or three years.

KEY FACTS

Min Temp -20°C (-4°F)
Soil Tolerates any soil type, as long as it is well-drained. Particularly happy in chalk
Site Happy anywhere – but the sunnier the spot, the denser the foliage
Vigour *L. lucidum* is a fast-growing tree, quickly reaching 4m (13ft) and ultimately approaching around 8m (25ft)

Care: This plant appreciates lots of moisture, especially for its first two seasons after planting. A few generous handfuls of blood, fish and bone around the base in mid-spring gives excellent results. It is also generally trouble-free from pests and diseases, although you should watch out for cats as they love to scratch the bark!

LOBELIA TUPA

Devil's tobacco

This huge perennial herb is at its most striking when planted in large numbers. Its towering spikes consist of thick stems covered with soft foliage on the bottom half, and have a magnificent spire of flowers on the top half. Leaves are pointed, downy and 25cm (10in) long. The flowers, which appear during midsummer, are made up of hundreds of tubular blooms that are deep red in colour.

Despite its size, *Lobelia tupa* stands up well against sea breezes, which makes it a good choice for a coastal garden. It also fits in with most other styles of gardening, but is hopeless in a pot so must be planted directly into the ground as soon as it is large enough to handle. Small plants are best introduced to the garden in the spring when that year's frosts have finished. In their first year, they will grow about 1m (3ft) – it is during their second year, however, that their full stature develops.

KEY FACTS

Min Temp -10°C (14°F)
Soil *Lobelia tupa* prefers rich, moist, fertile and free-draining soil
Site Will grow well in full sun or light shade
Vigour This plant can reach up to 2m (6½ft) tall

Care: Water plants well during the growing season from late spring until early autumn. Feed with well-rotted manure annually in early spring. Remove dead flower spikes when they turn brown. Green aphids can be a problem on the growing tips.

LYONOTHAMNUS FLORIBUNDUS ASPLENIIFOLIUS

The Santa Cruz ironwood tree

A beautiful evergreen tree that has soft ferny leaves, dark red craggy bark and a ridiculously long name. The leaves are bright green and rough to the touch. When the weather is either dry and frosty or extremely hot and sunny, the foliage gives off a pleasant marshmallow aroma. In its early years, all the energy seems to go into reaching a decent height. The bark does not develop its gnarled rugged look for several years.

This tree, lovely as it may be, is a bit of a fusspot. Its ideal location would be in the lee of a warm, sunny wall. The support of a strong stake when newly planted is essential, and will be needed for at least three years.

KEY FACTS

Min Temp -10°C (14°F)
Soil Neutral to acid preferred. Tolerates alkaline soil if lime content is not excessive
Site Full sun in a sheltered spot. In frost-prone areas, shelter from cold, drying winds
Vigour Fast-growing, it can reach 5m (16½ft) in five years. Its ultimate height rarely exceeds 8m (25ft)

Care: Water this tree regularly for its first few seasons. Once it is established, irrigation is unnecessary. A mix of blood, fish and bone each spring should keep it looking healthy. It responds well to light pruning and is also relatively pest- and disease-free, so long as it is planted in the ground rather than being confined to a pot.

MAGNOLIA GRANDIFLORA   *Bull bay*

Often grown as a large wall shrub, it is far superior as a free-standing plant. This magnificent evergreen tree has huge leaves that are dark green and glossy on the surface and dusted reddish-brown underneath. The flowers are massive cream cups that are heavily fragrant. Each flower only lasts a few days, but mature trees produce a continuous supply for many weeks.

KEY FACTS
Min Temp -20°C (-4°F)
Soil Any – will even grow on alkaline soil
Site Full sun or light shade in a sheltered position preferred
Vigour This plant will grow up to around 9m (30ft) and its flowers are massive – up to 30cm (1ft) across

CARE: This plant appreciates adequate moisture, but not a boggy site. Feed it well with blood, fish and bone in mid-spring. Branches can be cut back ruthlessly in mid-spring. Usually pest- and disease-free.

MELIANTHUS MAJOR

Honey flower or honey bush

A highly decorative perennial with huge, deeply cut foliage. The leaves are beautifully sculpted, pale blue-grey in colour and exude a strong smell of peanut butter when they are touched. Mature plants send up tall flower spikes that are best described as interesting and spectacular, rather than beautiful.

The spikes soar above the foliage and open up into slender cone shapes that are coloured blood red. The flowering period is usually around early summer. The outer parts of the flowers contain a honey-like substance, hence the common name of 'honey flower'.

The size and colour of the leaves of this plant contrast very well with virtually all the other architectural plants, whether they are trees, bamboos or herbaceous.

This plant is hopeless in a pot unless it is grown in a truly gigantic container. It is therefore best to plant it in the ground if at all possible.

KEY FACTS

Min Temp - 4°C (24°F)
Soil Rich, moist and fertile. Well-drained loam would be ideal
Site Full sun or light shade in a sheltered spot away from strong winds
Vigour A height of at least 1.5m (5ft) can be reached within one year – most of the growth occurs in the autumn

CARE: Moist conditions are preferred. Remove older leaves when they get brown and crispy. Stems are delicate, so use secateurs to make clean cuts. Can be pruned back to ground level – the new growth will take a while to appear. This plant is usually problem-free.

MUSA BASJOO *Japanese hardy banana*

This is definitely the most absurd-looking exotic tropical plant that can be grown in colder climates. Its leaves grow from a base that eventually forms a fibrous, watery trunk. Suckers are produced from around this base and grow to form a small grove of extra plants. Mature stems can produce flowers that are large and lumpy. Behind the flower bud, tiny bunches of bananas appear. These are hard, green and inedible but truly amazing.

Flowering stems die after fruiting, but send up new plants from the roots. Frost always destroys the foliage. In milder gardens, the trunk stays hardy through the winter and new growth starts from the top the following year. In colder areas the trunk can be left for the frost to kill and new growth will appear from the base the following late spring. Alternatively, the trunk can be wrapped up for the winter (*see* pp 20–21). By doing this, it remains alive all winter and new growth will then sprout from the top. This produces a bigger plant.

KEY FACTS
Min Temp -10°C (14°F)
Soil Rich, moist and fertile soil is best
Site Light shade is preferred, in a sheltered spot
Vigour The plant can reach 2m (6½ft) in one year and over time may grow to 6m (20ft)

CARE: Vast amounts of water required throughout the growing season. Feed every four weeks from mid-spring to midsummer with well-rotted manure or a mix of blood, fish and bone. Diseases are not usually a problem unless the plant is stressed by being forced to grow in a pot.

MYRTUS LUMA

Orange bark myrtle

The soft, suede-like orange bark makes this tree irresistible to the touch. Its colour varies in intensity throughout the year. During the summer, the bark splits and peels to reveal patches of creamy white that gradually darken and change back to orange again. Young plants do not have the characteristic orange bark. This will start to appear after about five years. The foliage is a dense mass of tiny, evergreen leaves that are aromatic when crushed. Fragrant white flowers appear from midsummer until mid-autumn, followed by large, fat fruits. These are black, juicy and edible.

This tree has been reliably reported as being able to grow in bogs. It is also a good candidate for topiary. It has a variety of different names and can appear on plant lists as *M. apiculata*, *Eugenia apiculata* or even *Myrceugenia apiculata* to name just a few.

Myrtus luma

KEY FACTS

Min Temp -10°C (14°F)
Soil Happiest in well-drained, fertile conditions
Site Sun or shade in a sheltered spot away from cold winds
Vigour Away from its native South America, expect an ultimate height of no more than 8m (25ft)

CARE: *Myrtus luma* is extremely intolerant of drought, so needs constant irrigation. Feed just enough to keep the foliage a good dark green colour. This species is not prone to any particular pest or disease.

OPHIOPOGON PLANISCAPUS 'NIGRESCENS'

Black grass

This is a plant that would please even the most design-conscious gardener. The leaves really are jet black. Although its small size means that it could easily be overlooked if just one or two are planted, a large drift of this lovely grass makes a stunning display – looking particularly effective in beds mulched with coloured grit or stones.

The almost unpronounceable *Ophiopogon planiscapus* 'Nigrescens' is evergreen, and has attractive sprigs of lilac flowers in late summer which are followed by small, shiny black berries that last for months.

As with all plants, it performs much better when planted directly into the ground, but will also live quite happily in a pot for many years. It is an unfussy plant that is virtually maintenance free.

KEY FACTS

Min Temp -20°C (-4°F)

Soil Light, sandy and well-drained

Site Full sun is preferred, in a sheltered position, but it also tolerates partial shade

Vigour The coal-coloured clumps slowly spread to cover areas of no more than 1m (3ft) with a maximum height of 15cm (6in)

CARE: This type of grass is fairly drought tolerant once established. Feed with a small amount of general fertiliser in mid-spring but the plant is generally easy to care for. Usually trouble-free but check for aphids during summer.

PAULOWNIA TOMENTOSA

The Foxglove tree

There are two ways to grow this plant. By leaving it to grow naturally, it will develop into a small tree. Branches form a neat, open canopy and the fragrant, pinkish-purple flowers are borne in late spring. The second method involves chopping the plant down hard each year in early spring. Although this prevents it from flowering, compensation is given in the form of gigantic leaves.

KEY FACTS

Min Temp -20°C (-4°F)
Soil Rich, fertile and well-drained soil is preferred
Site Light shade is best, in a sheltered position
Vigour If grown as a tree, this plant will reach around 8m (25ft). If cut back, it will grow 3m (10ft) each year

CARE: Copious amounts of water needed during the growing season. Feed heavily every four weeks from mid-spring until midsummer. Capsid bug can be a menace.

PHORMIUM COOKIANUM   *Mountain flax*

Sword-shaped, evergreen leaves grow from fan-shaped bases in copious amounts, making a strongly architectural shape for the garden. Flower spikes are sent up from the centre during the summer. They are slightly taller than the foliage, and would be referred to as interesting rather than items of stunning loveliness. They open out into large yellowish-green angular blooms and when these fade, seed pods begin to form which are much more attractive than the flowers and should be left on the plant to enjoy visually. They are long-lasting and much admired.

The plant is sometimes still listed under the synonym of *P. colensoi*. The variegated form, *P. cookianum* 'Tricolor', has striking leaves of cream and green with subtle red edges and it is just as hardy.

KEY FACTS

Min Temp -10°C (14°F)

Soil Fertile and free-draining. In frost-prone areas, supply a deep, dry mulch

Site Full sun or light shade – this plant is excellent for growing in exposed coastal gardens

Vigour *Phormium cookianum* grows to 1.2m (4ft) tall and wide within three years

CARE: Water the plant well for the first season. Watering after then is only needed in periods of drought. Feed annually with blood, fish and bone. Don't plant the central base too low – water gathers there, leading to rotting. Mealy bug can be a problem, but apart from this pest the plant is relatively trouble-free.

PHORMIUM TENAX *New Zealand flax*

Massive sword-shaped leaves up to 2m (6½ft) tall grow from fan-shaped bases to create enormous clumps of upright foliage. This is an easy plant to cultivate and has been the basis for many architectural gardens for years. The flower spikes are extraordinary – they tower over the foliage by many feet and open up into angular, reddish-brown flowers. The flowers remarkably still manage to look quite attractive even when they are dead and their colour has faded and turned black.

The variegated version, *P. tenax* 'Variegatum' is worthy of a mention even though it is slightly less hardy. This grows to 1.8m (6ft) tall. There is also a good purple variety, *P. tenax purpureum*, which is even less hardy and grows to around 1.5m (5ft) tall. There are hundreds of other named cultivars available, all with brightly coloured foliage. Few are hardy and within

CARE: Water the plant well for the first season. Watering after that time is only needed during periods of drought. Feed annually with blood, fish and bone. Don't plant the central base too low – water gathers there, leading to rotting. Mealy bug can be a problem, but apart from this pest the plant is relatively trouble-free.

two years most
of them will either
be dead or have
reverted to a mucky
brown colour.
They are probably
best regarded
as temporary
bedding plants.

KEY FACTS
Min Temp
-20°C (-4°F)
Soil Fertile and
free-draining. In
frost-prone areas,
supply a deep,
dry mulch
Site Full sun or
light shade – the
plant is an excellent
choice for exposed
coastal gardens
Vigour A mature
clump could
grow to be 2.5m
(8ft) across within
six years

PHYLLOSTACHYS AUREA   *Golden bamboo*

Apart from being a fine-looking bamboo, *P. aurea* is also an extremely versatile plant. It has thick canes with attractive knobbly bits on them and masses of delicate-looking foliage. It has a very vertical habit and stays in tight clumps at the base, making it suitable for even the smallest of gardens. It is a brilliant plant for screening purposes. Because it is non-invasive, it could just about qualify as a suitable candidate for a pot, providing the container is enormous and has automatic irrigation.

Despite its common name, the canes usually remain green, except in very hot climates, when they can take on a golden hue. Avoid planting in a windy position to ensure that the foliage remains green and healthy.

KEY FACTS

Min Temp -20°C (-4°F)

Soil Fertile, manure-enriched clay soil

Site Full sun or light shade, in a position sheltered from the wind

Vigour Maximum height is unlikely to be more than 5m (16½ft)

CARE: Never allow this plant to dry out, especially during its first few seasons. Feed with a mix of blood, fish and bone or any high-nitrogen feed every four weeks from mid-spring until early summer. Bamboo canes never get any thicker, so it is a good idea to cut out all thin or weak-looking canes as soon as they appear. Remove older brown leaves as they appear. Aphids like this plant.

PHYLLOSTACHYS AUREOSULCATA 'AUREOCAULIS'

This is one of the most attractive bamboos. New canes are tinged a lovely pinkish-red colour that gradually ripens to a deep butter yellow. As with many of the *Phyllostachys* bamboos, the clumps stay nice and tight at the base, so that even the smallest town garden could accommodate one of these remarkable plants.

The leaves are tiny and massed in such quantity that they can be clipped to form a hedge. Single specimens look rather interesting if trimmed lightly up the sides with the crown shaped into a rounded dome. However, they can also be left to grow naturally and enjoyed as they are.

Propagation is not that easy for the amateur gardener, but dividing a specimen up into sections in early spring might occasionally be successful.

KEY FACTS

Min Temp -20°C (-4°F)

Soil Rich, fertile and moisture-retentive soil is preferred

Site Full sun produces the best-coloured canes. Provide the plant with protection from very strong winds

Vigour Canes are produced at an extraordinarily prolific rate – around 80 in just five years. The height, however is only likely to reach 5m (16½ft)

CARE: Must never be allowed to dry out, especially before becoming well established. Feed with a high-nitrogen feed from mid-spring to early summer. Remove any new foliage that appears outside the main clump to maintain a neat and tidy appearance. Check the growing tips regularly for aphids during the spring and summer.

PHYLLOSTACHYS NIGRA   *Black bamboo*

Although the foliage of *Phyllostachys nigra* is perfectly acceptable, it is the canes that make this bamboo so popular. Mature clumps have numerous straight, thick black canes that many gardeners find irresistible. After a shower of rain, they become darker and glossier and even more beautiful.

This bamboo prefers a sheltered position completely out of the wind and also out of the way of people brushing past it. If planted in an exposed site, the small leaves quickly become desiccated and brown around the edges.

New canes are quite green at first and gradually ripen to their ebony colour after the full height is reached. To speed up the process, canes can be chopped off at 2.5m (8ft). This does no harm – it just produces a shorter, much more manageable plant.

KEY FACTS

Min Temp -20°C (-4°F)

Soil Growing this plant in fertile, manure-enriched clay soil gives excellent results

Site Full sun or light shade, sheltered from the wind

Vigour This is a slow plant to get going, but once the roots are fully established growth accelerates rapidly. Individual specimens can reach 5m (16¹⁄₂ft) with a spread of 1m (3ft) after six to eight years

CARE: Permanent access to water is essential. Several handfuls of a blood, fish and bone mix sprinkled around the base every four weeks from mid-spring until early summer are also beneficial. Remove older brown leaves as they appear. Cut out any thin or weak-looking canes as soon as they appear too. Aphids are often a problem for this plant in spring and summer.

PINUS PATULA   *Mexican weeping pine*

A large, spreading tree that needs plenty of space around it to appreciate the long flowing lines of the branches. Branches start low down and almost drape the ground. They have a wide spread of at least 6m (20ft) from tip to tip and hang gracefully in layers

all the way up the tree. From each branch, elegant long needles of a brilliant emerald green are suspended, giving a very shaggy effect – almost like a green orang-utan. The trunk is attractive in its own right, being a craggy reddish brown, but this is nearly always hidden by the thick foliage.

This plant is reputed to be a lime-hater, but experience has proved this not to be so, if the lime content is not too excessive of course. What the tree hates most of all is strong, cold winds, which will turn the tips of the leaves brown. It also performs very badly in shade, resulting in an drawn open habit.

KEY FACTS

Min Temp -10°C (14°F)

Soil Very well-drained, loamy soil is preferred

Site Likes full sun in a sheltered position away from cold winds

Vigour Grows fairly fast – can reach 9m (30ft) in ten years, with an ultimate height of 15m (50ft)

CARE: Hates boggy conditions, but water regularly until established. Give an occasional light feed of blood, fish and bone mix in late spring if needed. It can be pruned regularly to look like a large bonsai if required. Pests and diseases are not usually a problem as long as the soil is well-drained.

PINUS PINEA   *Umbrella pine or stone pine*

This shapely round-headed evergreen tree is ideal for medium-sized gardens. Planted with *Cupressus sempervirens* it provides a real Mediterranean flavour. The trunk is rough and craggy and can become fairly stocky after just a few years. The head of foliage is a mass of soft, feathery pine needles. Large cones are regularly produced – these contain edible seeds that are sold as pine kernels.

This tree is perfect for growing in all sorts of hostile environments. It is suitable for planting as a single specimen or in small groves. Strong tree stakes are needed initially – keep in place for at least three years.

If large, container-grown trees are being planted, expect considerable leaf drop. This is a result of it being transplanted but by the following season, growth should be lush once more.

KEY FACTS
Min Temp -20°C (-4°F)
Soil Grows well whether in clay, flint, chalk, loam or even poor, sandy soil
Site Full sun. Copes well with strong coastal winds
Vigour The height eventually matches the width of its head – around 5m (16½ft) after 15 years

CARE: Hates boggy conditions, but water it for its first two seasons until established. To get the roots off to a good start, sprinkle bonemeal into the planting hole. Don't feed it for several years unless the soil is really poor. This ensures that all the energy is concentrated on the root system, which must be strong enough to support the wide crown. Gradually saw off the lower branches in order to raise the crown and keep the head rounded. The plant is trouble-free.

Pittosporum tobira

PITTOSPORUM TOBIRA

Japanese mock orange

One of the most versatile plants available, *P. tobira* can be trained as a small tree, clipped into a hedge or left as a shapely shrub. The dwarf form can be grown in a pot. Flowers are borne in clusters during late spring and early summer, and they have a heady perfume. After a hot summer, these are followed by bunches of green seedpods. When ripe, the pods split open to reveal bright orange seeds.

P. tobira is fantastically salt-resistant and makes an excellent addition to a coastal garden.

KEY FACTS
Min Temp -10°C (14°F)
Soil Any – best in fertile, moist and well-drained soil
Site Sun or shade – excellent in exposed windy gardens
Vigour Ultimate height is not usually more than 2.5m (8ft)

CARE: Once established this plant is drought resistant. Prune shaped plants or hedging in early spring or right after flowering. Black aphids can be a menace.

PODOCARPUS SALIGNUS   *Willow podocarp*

Shaggy heaps of luxurious, emerald green, willow-like foliage make this beautiful evergreen conifer one of the most essential additions to any garden, especially one with exotic tendencies. It is much hardier than generally described and can survive severe winters if grown in a protected spot sheltered from cold winds.

Although the plant's bark is usually hidden behind the dense foliage, it is attractive in its own right, being reddish-brown, fibrous and peeling off in strips. Small red berries are occasionally produced.

Podocarpus salignus prefers to be grown away from other plants as it does not like to compete for food and moisture. Bear this in mind when you plant it out.

KEY FACTS

Min Temp -20°C (-4°F)
Soil Neutral to acid preferred, although alkaline conditions can be coped with
Site Likes a sheltered spot in light shade, away from other trees and plants
Vigour Very slow to establish – takes two years for the roots to settle in, then new foliage is produced at a rate of 15–20cm (6–8in) each year. Its ultimate height of 15m (50ft) takes at least 20 years

CARE: The best results are produced by watering regularly enough to keep the soil moist but not boggy. A light mix of blood, fish and bone can be given in late spring. Too much food can scorch the ends of the leaves. Pruning is not necessary unless a hedge or smaller plant is required. Generally free from blight by pests and diseases.

PSEUDOPANAX CRASSIFOLIUS

The Lancewood

This plant is either loved passionately or loathed because it looks so strange. The trunk and branches are craggy, but dead straight – however it is for the leaves that this tree is considered peculiar. They are up to 60cm (2ft) long, only 1cm (½in) wide, almost black and look as if they are made of plastic. Sometimes they have an orange or red stripe running down the centre. The edges are sharply serrated. The leaves hang down at an angle of 45°, giving the tree an upside down look. The leaves go through several phases before reaching adulthood. With each one, the leaves become shorter, wider and greener until they look almost normal. They also stop hanging down vertically, gradually lifting upwards. The older foliage drops off over time.

This tree seems to have an almost non-existent root system, which makes it a good candidate for growing in a large pot.

KEY FACTS

Min Temp -10°C (14°F)
Soil Any
Site Full sun in a quiet, sheltered spot
Vigour A mature tree can reach around 6m (20ft) with a spread of only 2.5m (8ft)

CARE: Happy in dry conditions. Requires regular watering if grown in a container. No special care needed. However, may need pruning if kept under glass. Aphids are often a problem on new shoots, but otherwise trouble-free.